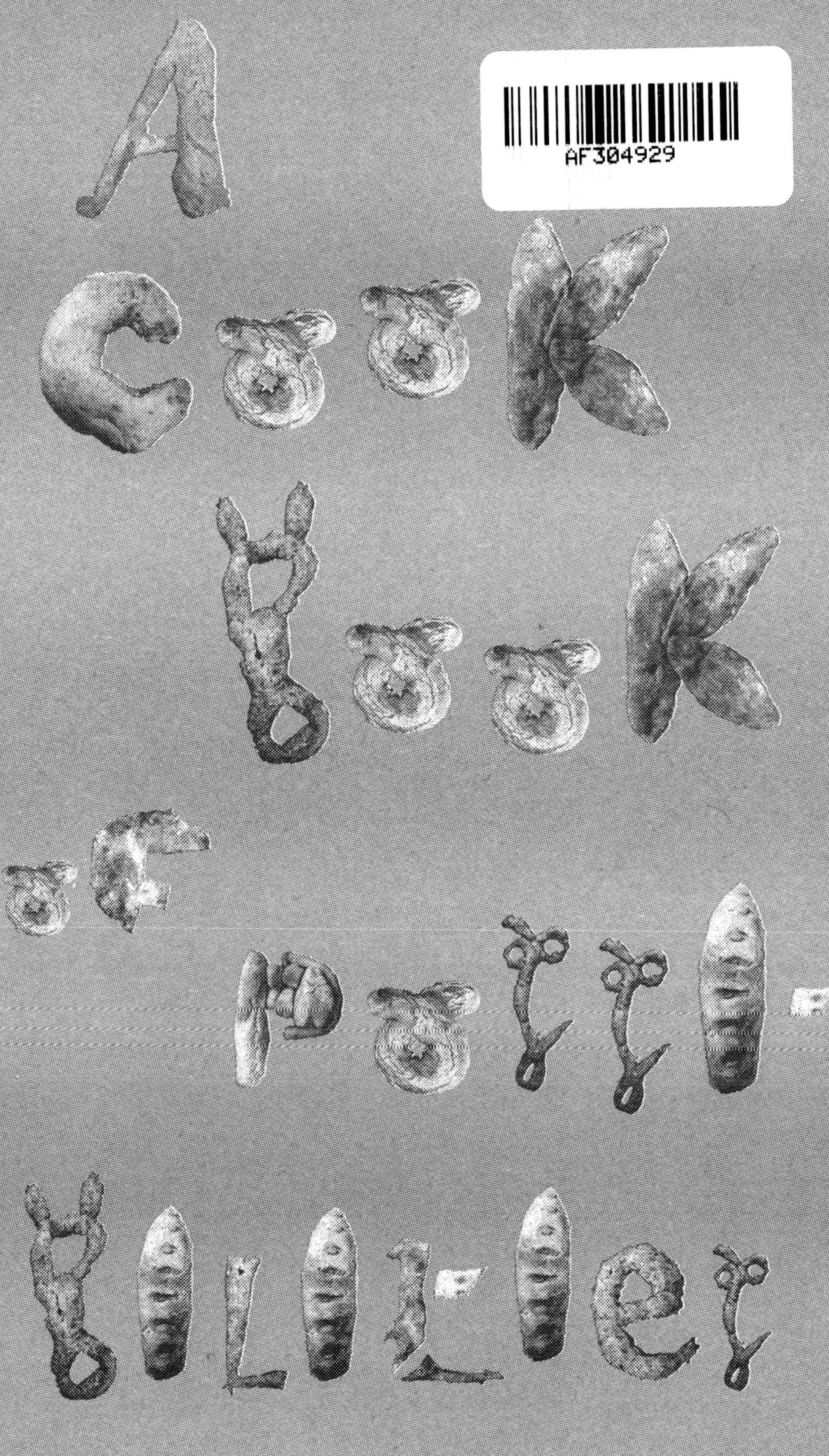
A COOK
BOOK
of Patti-
nuller

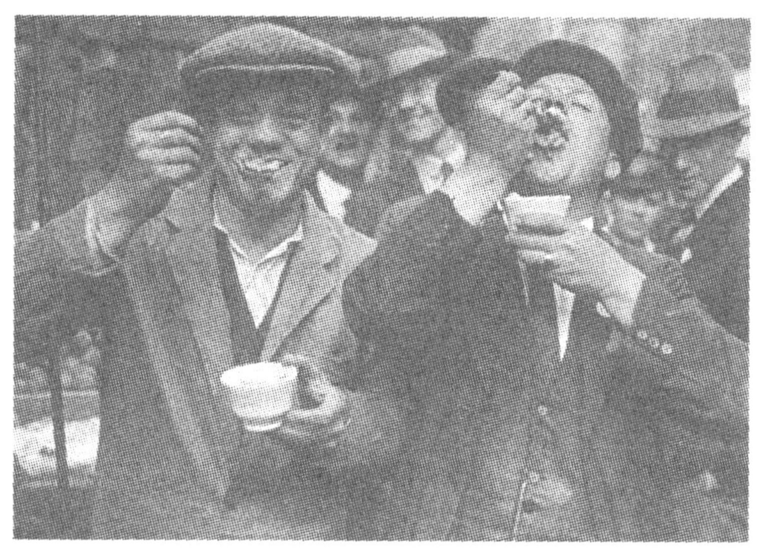

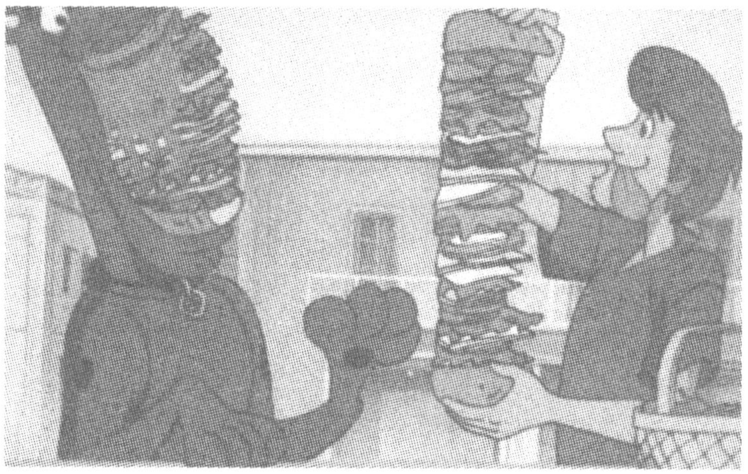

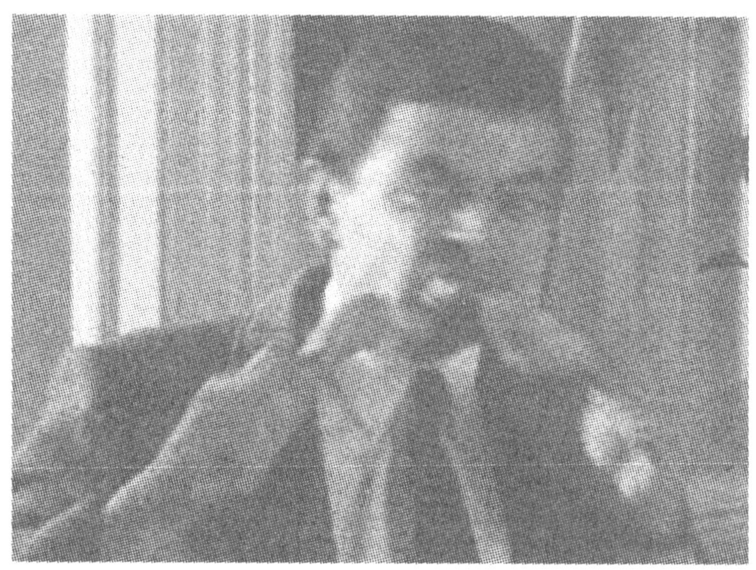

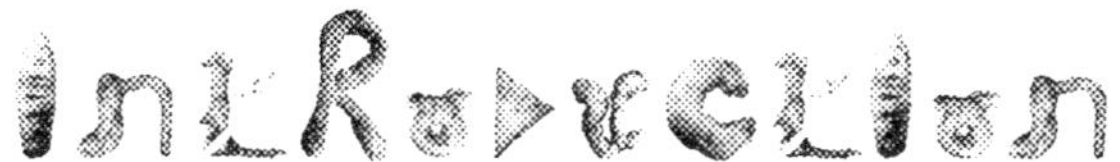

introduction

The starting point of many of Hato's projects has been food; the first publication we released was *Studio Cookbook* (2010), which collated recipes by other creative studios. Since then, we've led pickling workshops, printed with vegetables, and vegetable inks, made a cookbook of film stills (*Cooking with Scorsese*, 2014), and we have a studio lunch together every day.

The reason we are so interested in food as a subject, especially for a workshop with school pupils, is because it's unacademic. It helps form our community, friendships and relationship with the world in a way that is outside the realm of how and what we usually learn at school. Food is something that exists outside the school gates: a trip to the supermarket at lunch, or a fast food chain after school, a home-cooked dinner… Working with sixth formers presents a particular opportunity, because their school lives – to some extent dictated by the curriculum – are nearly over. They are beginning to think about the decisions that will define their future, about what interests them and about how to pursue their artistic talent in a difficult climate.

This publication takes its cue from *Parsons Bread Book* (1974), an alternative yearbook made up of final year design students' from the New York school's baking experiments (rather than autobiographical information or photos). The idea of making your own food and experiencing the craft of cooking can be empowering; during our project with Welling, the students baked bread letters, grew seeds, collected menus, compared food packaging and mascots, made drawings with grease, and divulged their fast food and coffee addictions. We encouraged the students to develop personal projects/proposals for this "cookbook" of ideas, while also being involved in the process of making a piece of design work: its concept, content, edit, design (typography) and production (risography). Bon appetit!

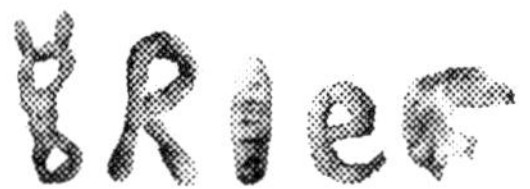

Food is a universal symbol and catalyst for the sharing and bringing together of people, friends and family. It carries its own culture, heritage and traditions, passed down from generation to generation.

We all have a personal relationship with food, whether through our daily routine or how we choose to cook and eat it. Cornflakes and apple juice, cheese and marmite sandwiches, a cup of tea with exactly one teaspoon of sugar at 7:30am? We want to know what food means to you. Does your Grandma keep secret recipes passed down from years before? Or have you created your own tradition?

Start by recording things in your sketchbook: write, photograph, draw and collect everything you can, no matter how related or abstract it is to your chosen subject; you never know how great the most useless of information can be! Think about the following areas and questions:

Culture
Are you part of a culture that's proud of its food tradition? For example, smoked jerk chicken cooked in an oil barrel. Do you know how to convert an oil barrel into a cooking device?

Friends & School
Do you and your friends eat out at a particular place? It could be a local bakery on the way to school, or your midnight snack? Do have any rituals before, during or after lessons or sports? For example eating oranges at half time.

At Home
Do you have any secret stashes of food at home? Do you eat a weird combination of food that no one else can understand? (Guy used to drink a pint of milk from the same beer mug with dinner everyday after school!)

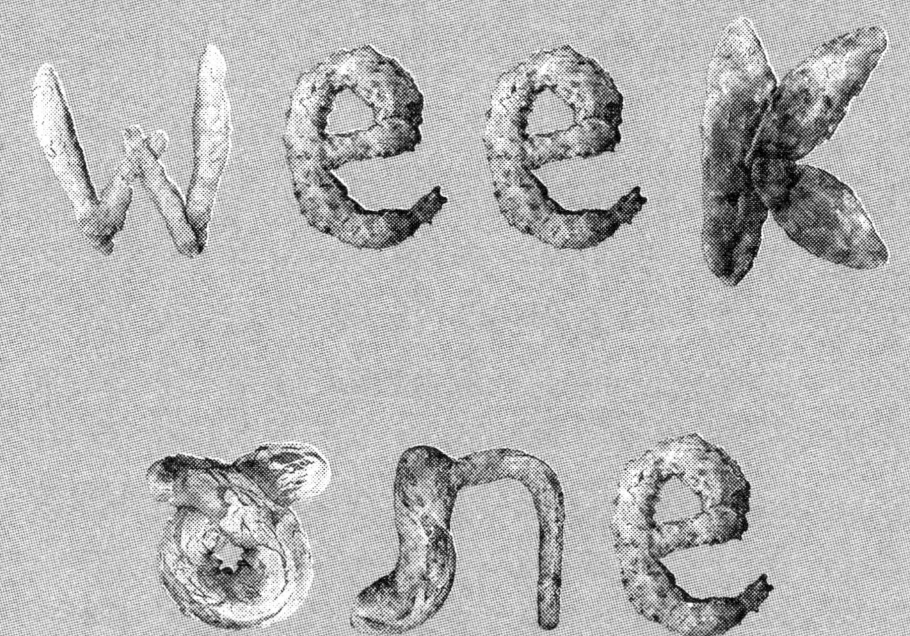
week
one

The students were asked to:

Interview three people
Family or friend
Someone you buy food/ingredients from
Someone you don't know

Ask them three to five questions
For example:
What's your favourite food?
What's the weirdest thing to eat?
Do you have any traditions/rituals?

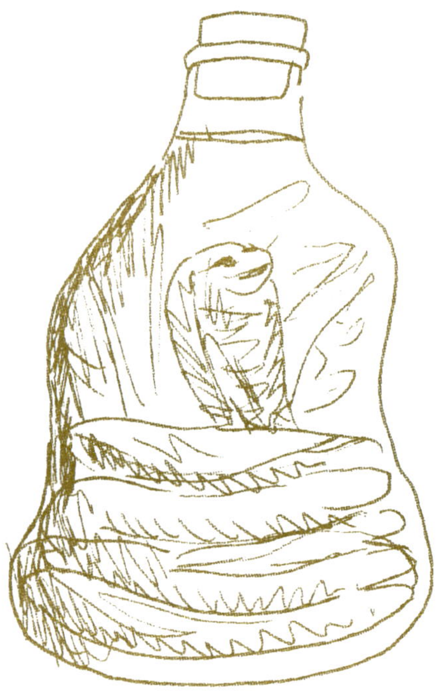

Halia

1) do italian + chinese
2) cake and chicken at once
3) dont know
4) NO
5) lasange + pasta
6) ~~nothing~~ chow pasta
7) marmite

8) No

Sami
1) sushi
2) tongue
3) market and super market
4) yes
5) microwave
6) chinese / scorpions
7) cous cous soup
8) yes

Bradley

1) Lasangra

2) cheese curry

3) ASDA

4) NO

5) Steak , spaggetti bolognuce

6) insects

7) cottage pie   — hate pie

8) yes

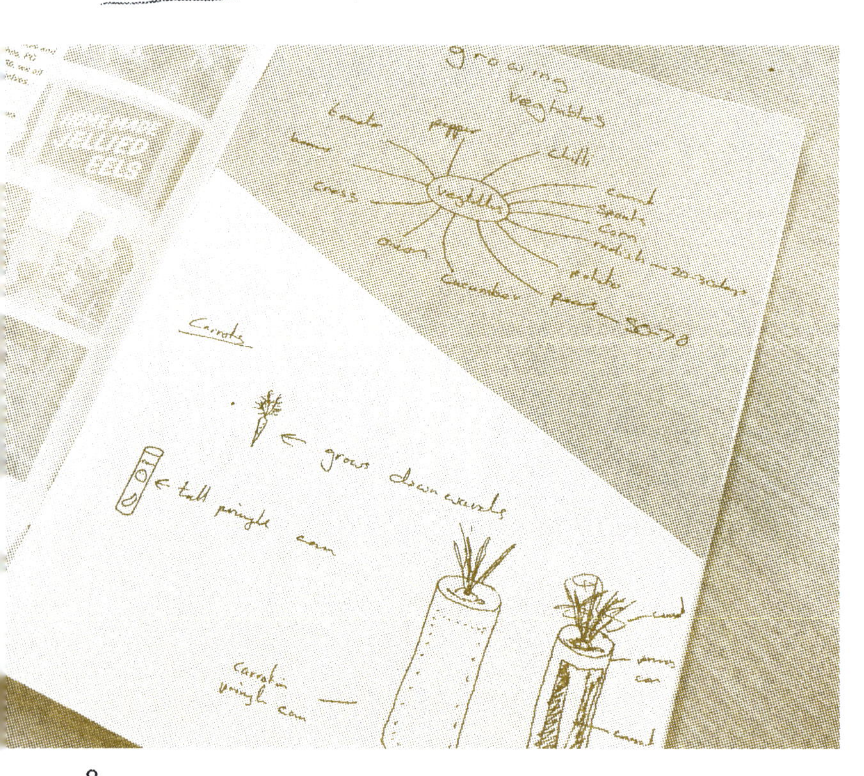

Food Interview

1) What is you favourite food?
Curry goat
Tofu
Pizza - cheesy bite

2) What is the weirdest food you have eaten?
Shark fin
muscles
grass

3) What is your worst food you have eaten?
Pork belly
Rubarb
spicey food

4) If you were a fruit, what one would you be?
Banana
Peach
Blueberry

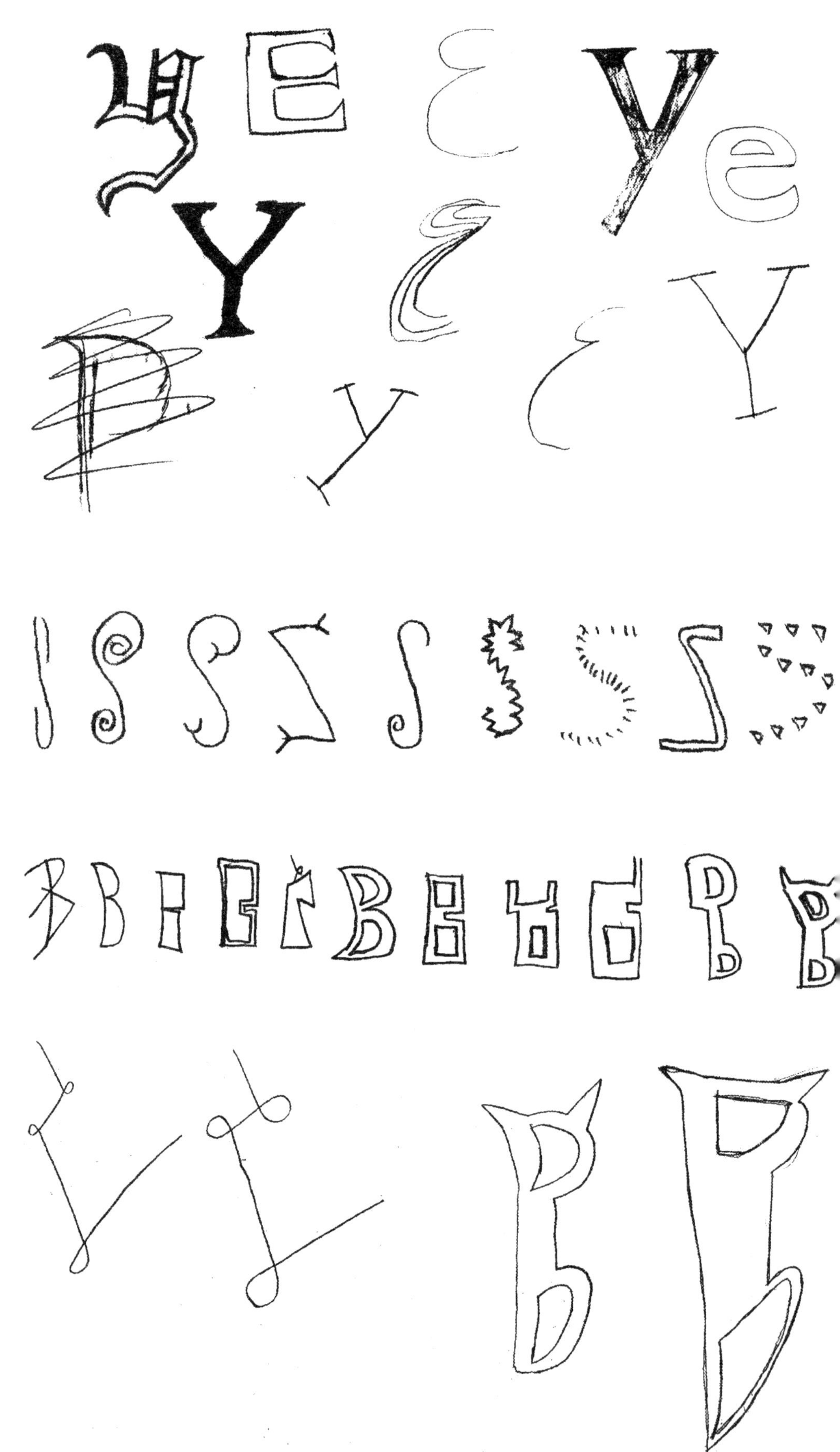

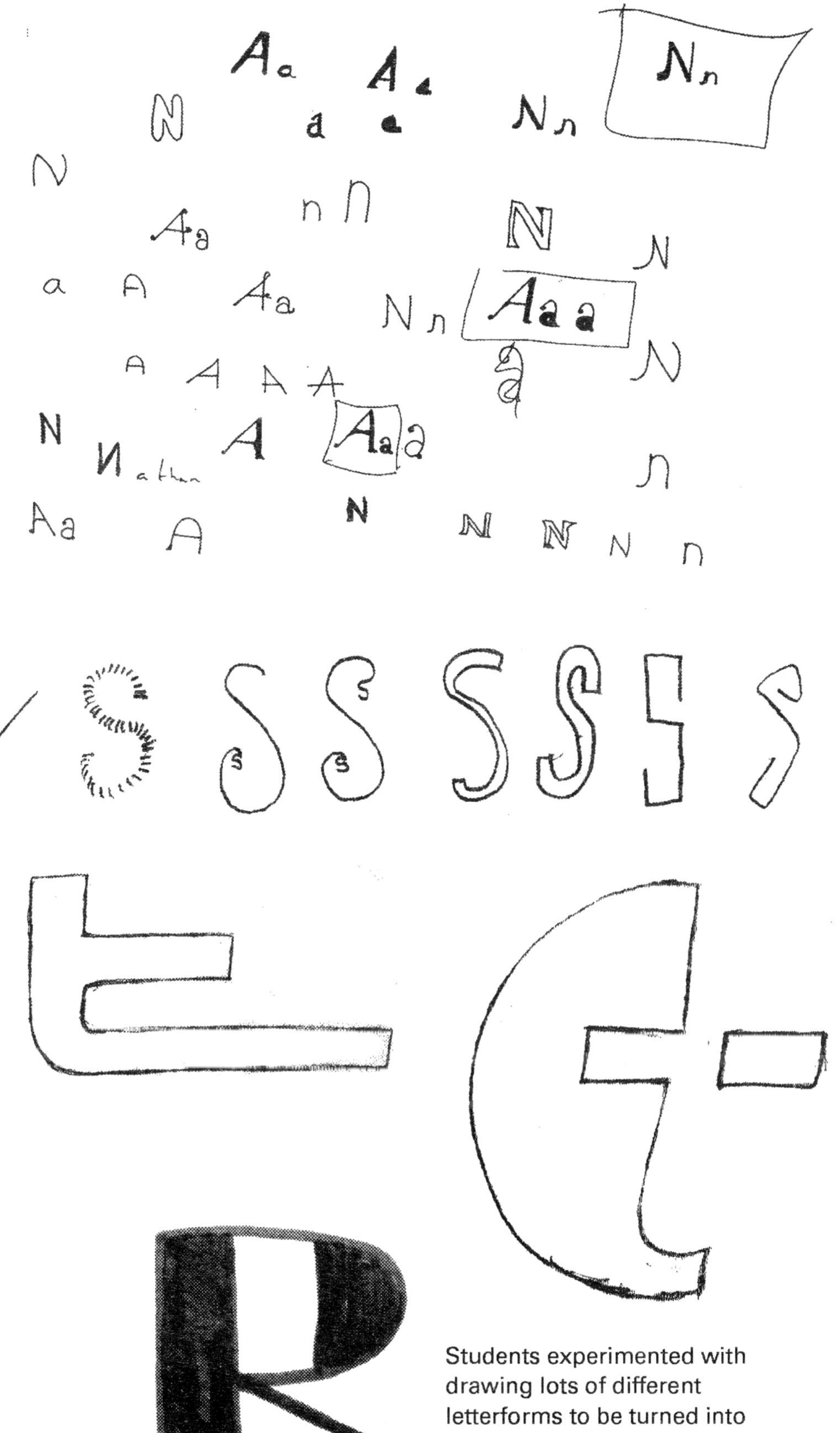

Students experimented with drawing lots of different letterforms to be turned into a bread font

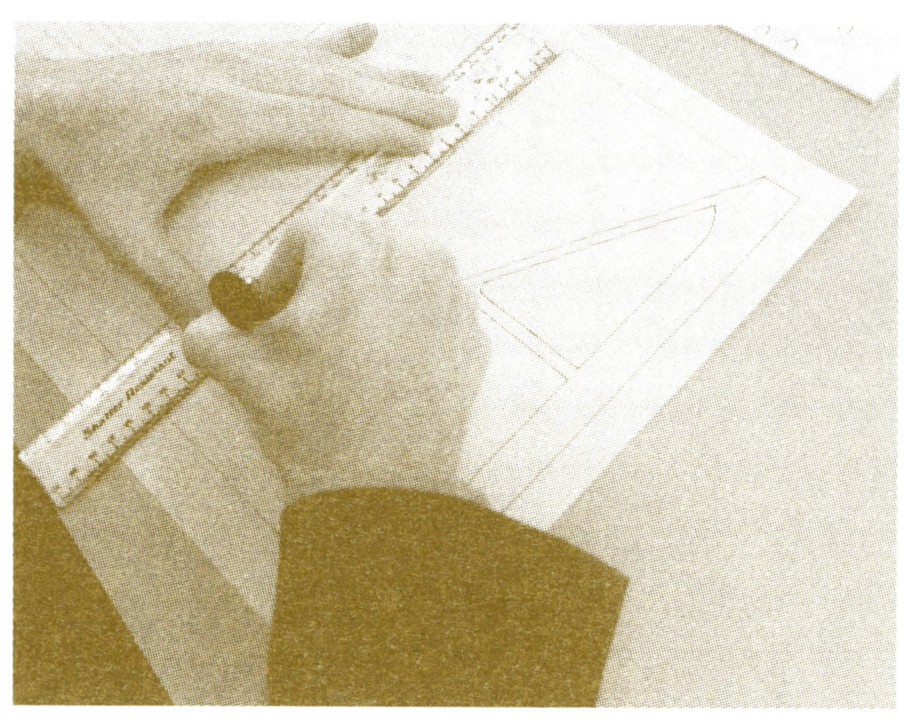

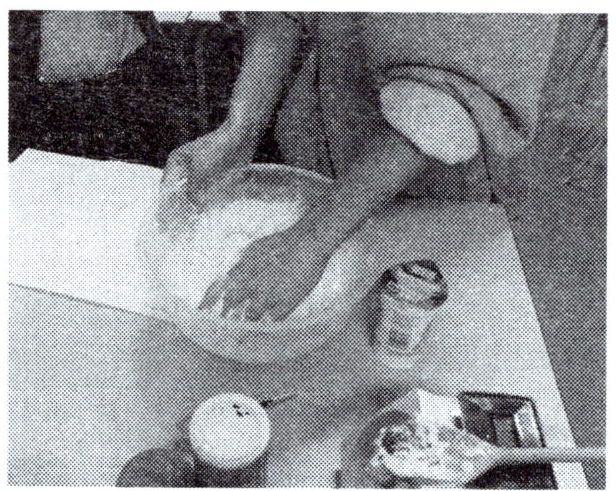

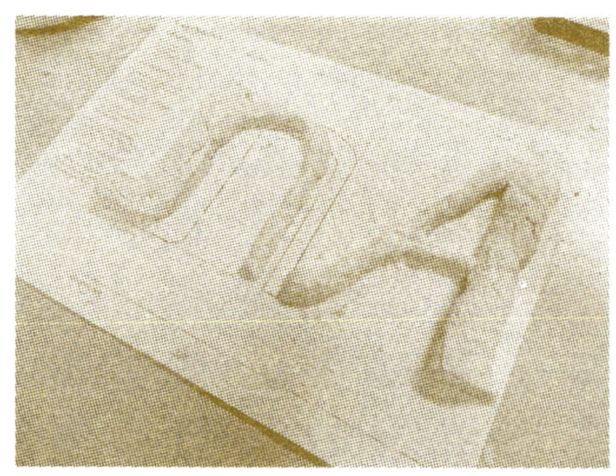

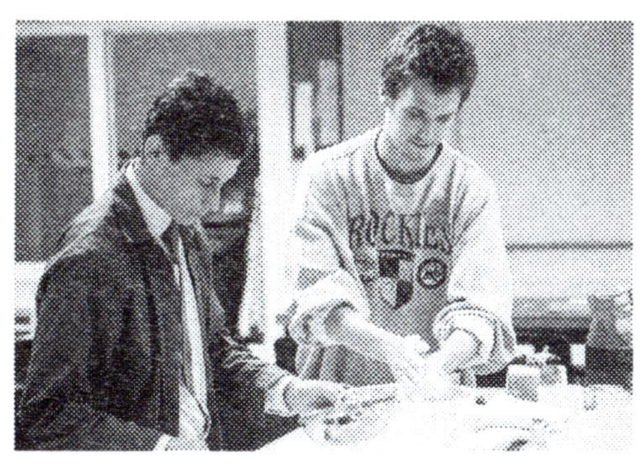

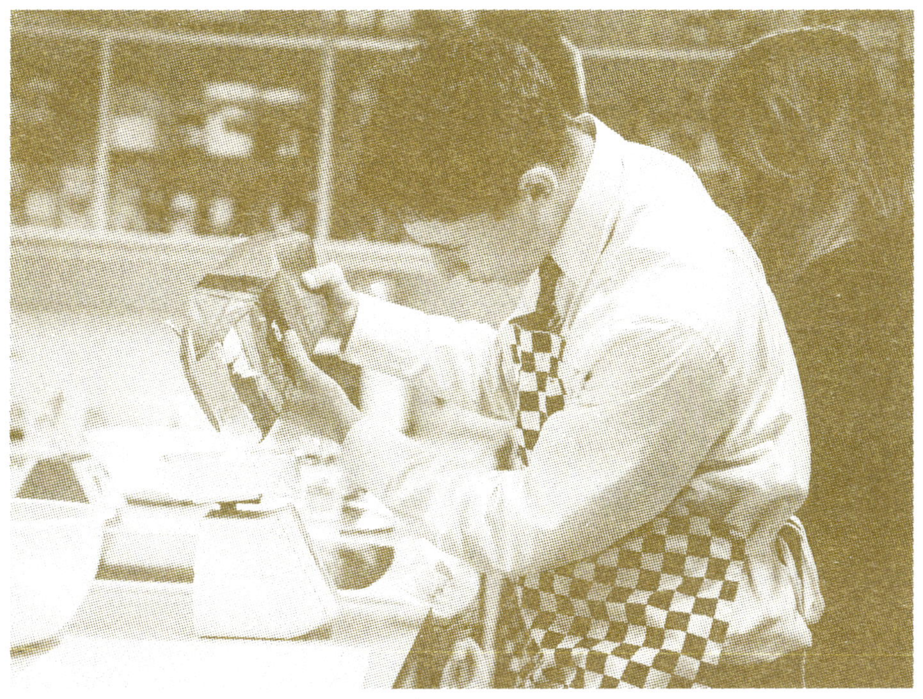

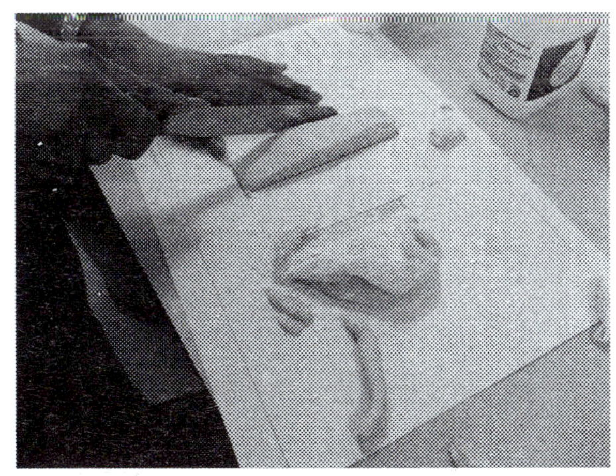

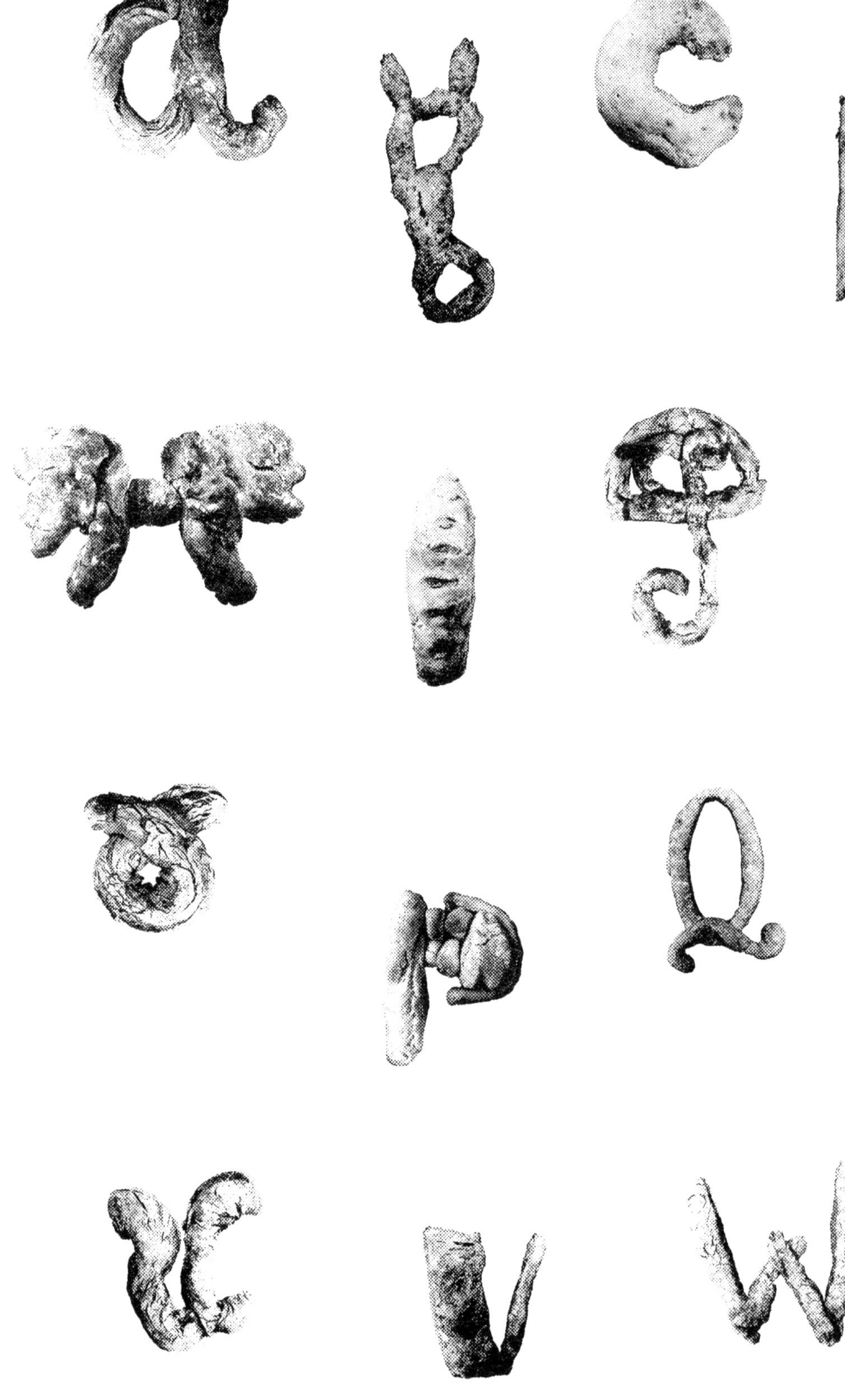

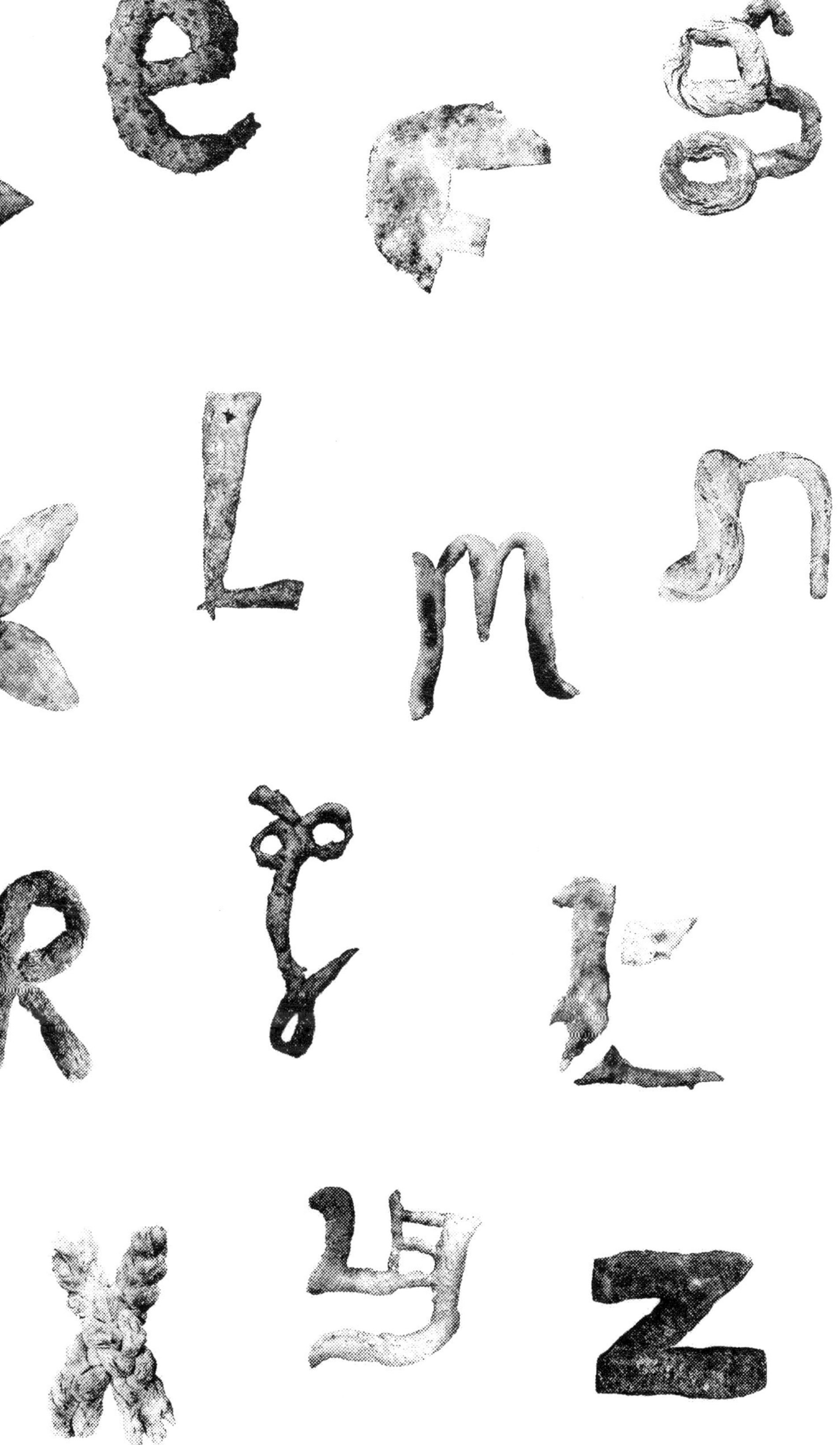

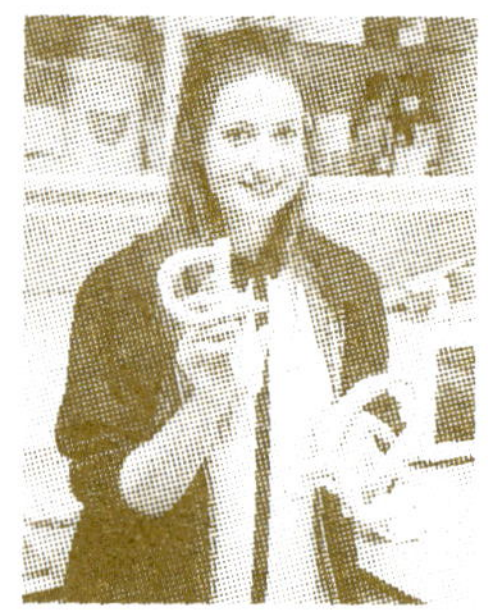

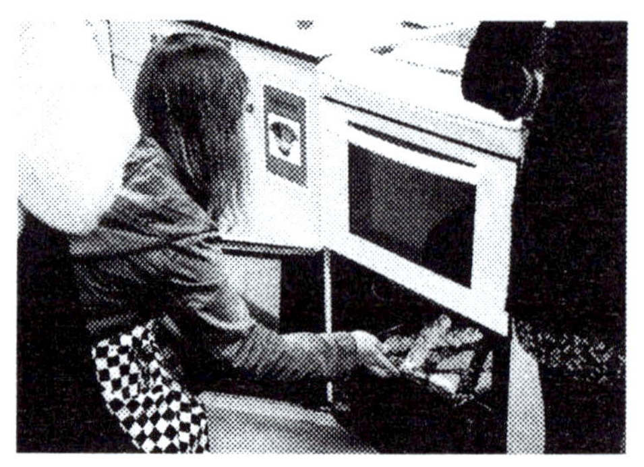

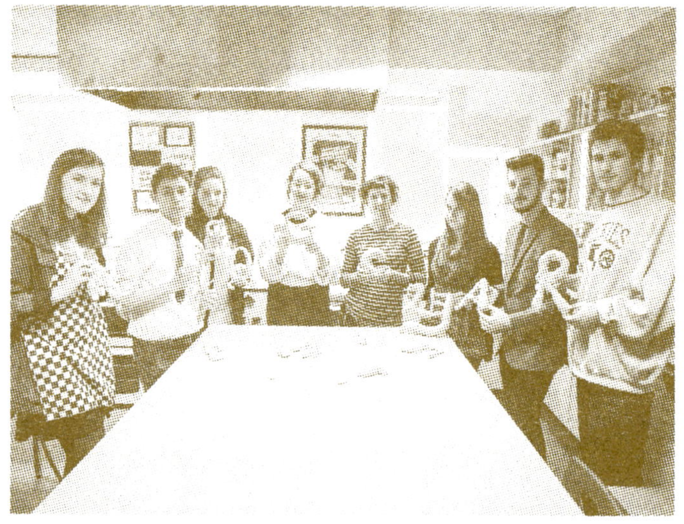

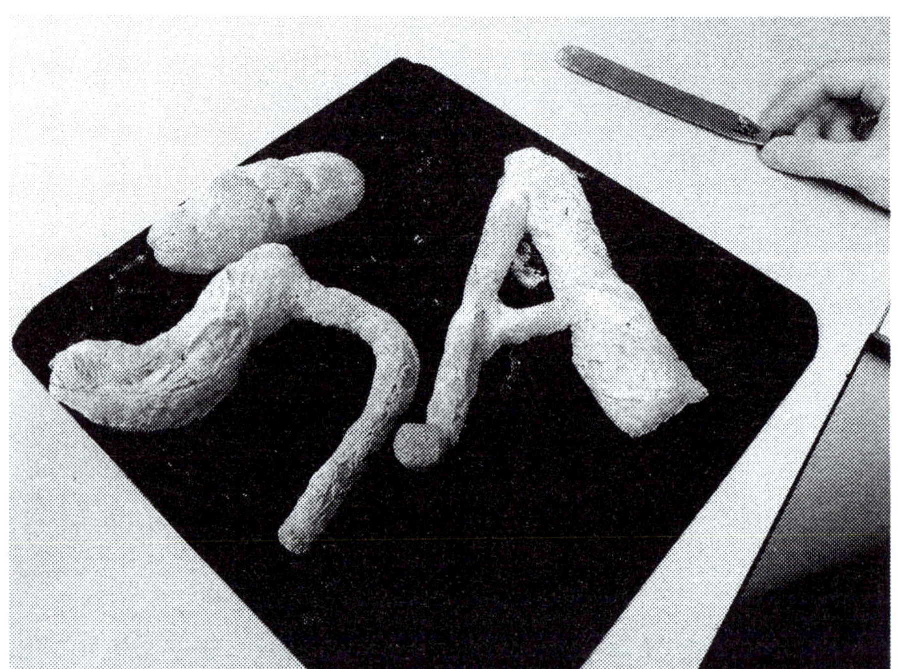

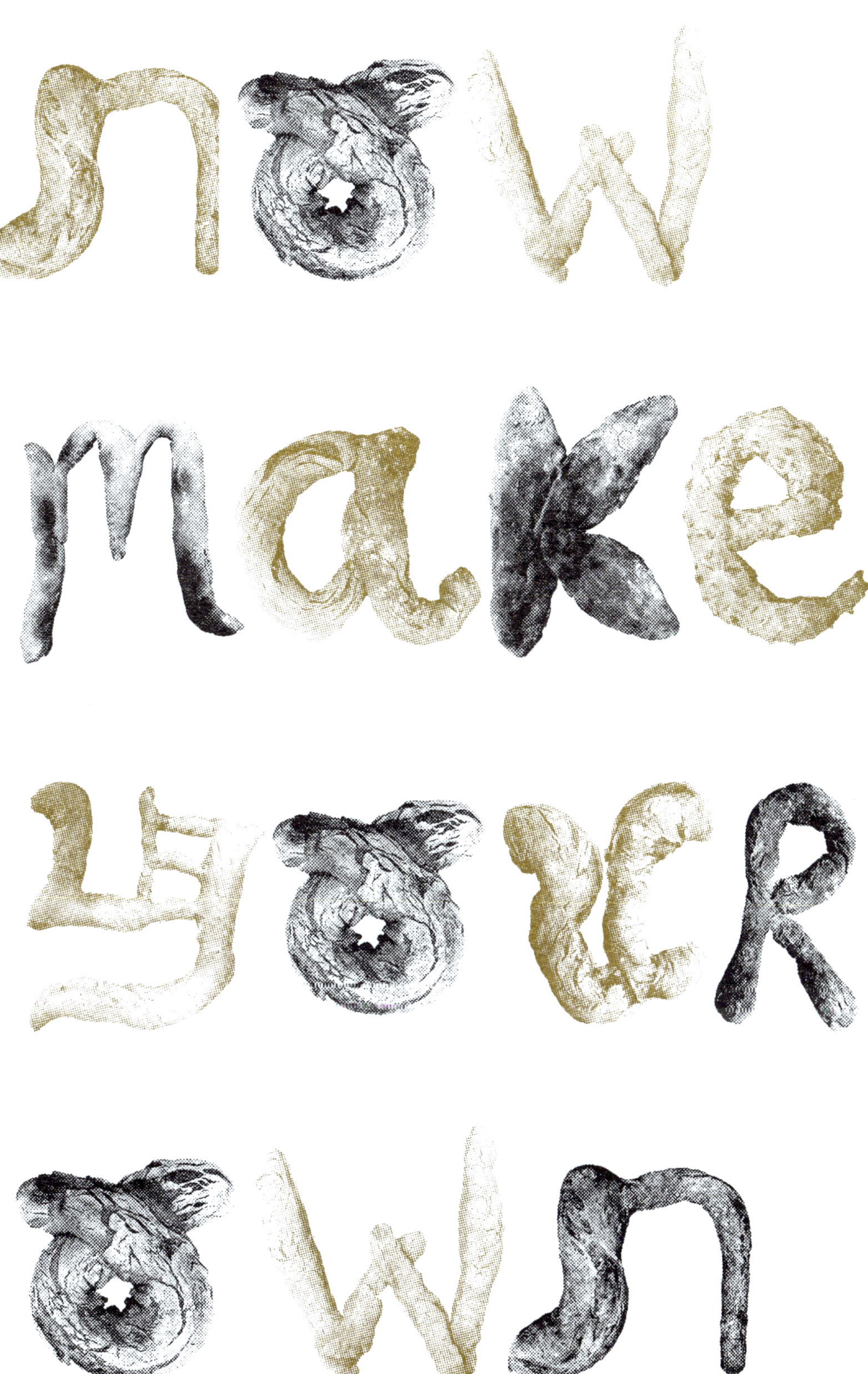

now
make
your
own

Ascender

X-Height

Baseline

Descender

Ingredients
130g Flour
1/2 tsp Salt
1/2 tsp Bicarbonate of Soda
145ml Buttermilk

Instructions
1. Measure out and mix the flour, salt and bicarbonate of soda together.

2. Make a well in the middle of the mixture.

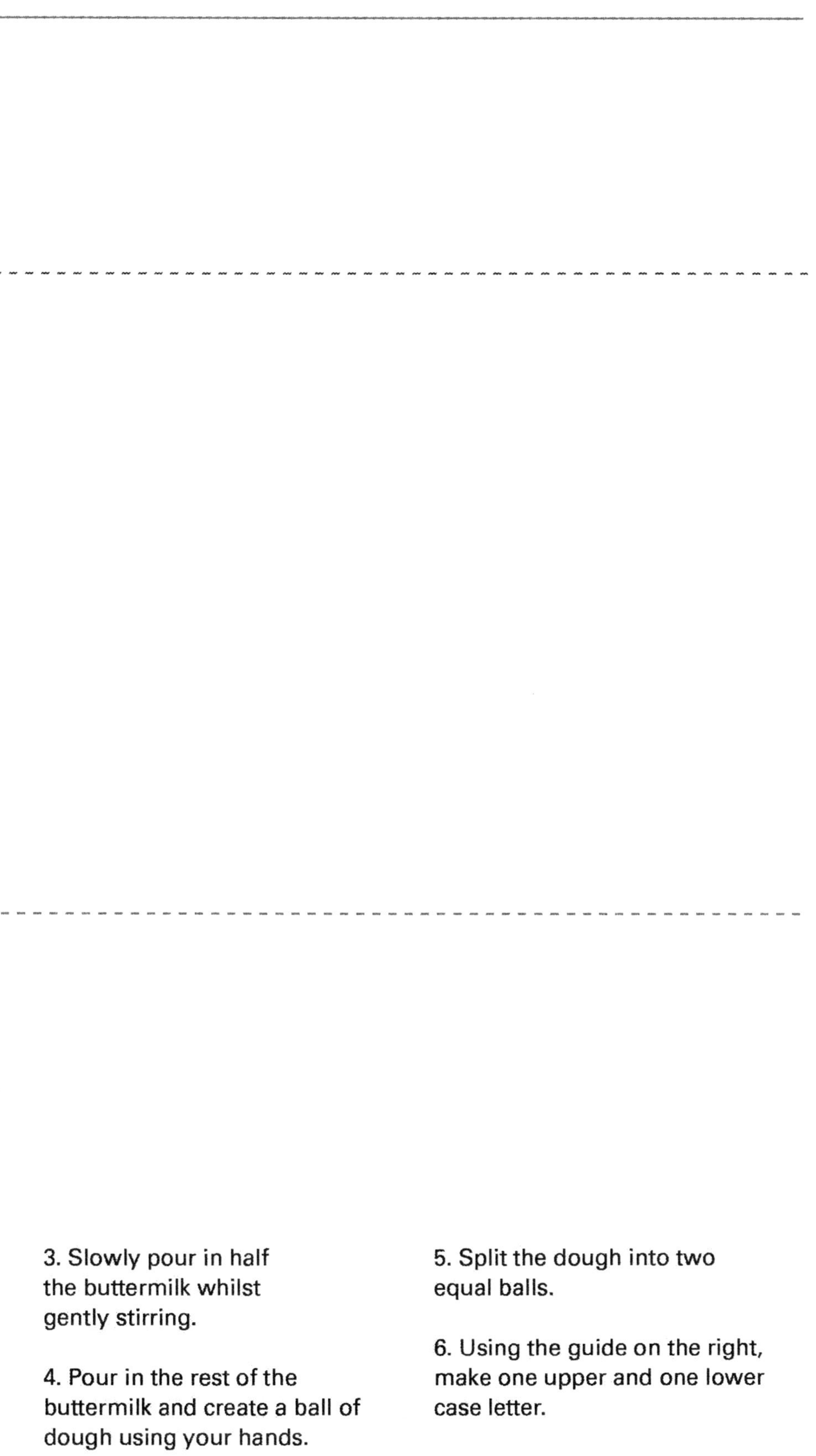

3. Slowly pour in half
the buttermilk whilst
gently stirring.

4. Pour in the rest of the
buttermilk and create a ball of
dough using your hands.

5. Split the dough into two
equal balls.

6. Using the guide on the right,
make one upper and one lower
case letter.

experiment

Cut out
illustrations
walk v. well

Collect
more
packaging?

>Line use
od Materials
>Experiment
more

Lots of ideas
that are
presented
well

I like the
anonyminity
of your
interviews

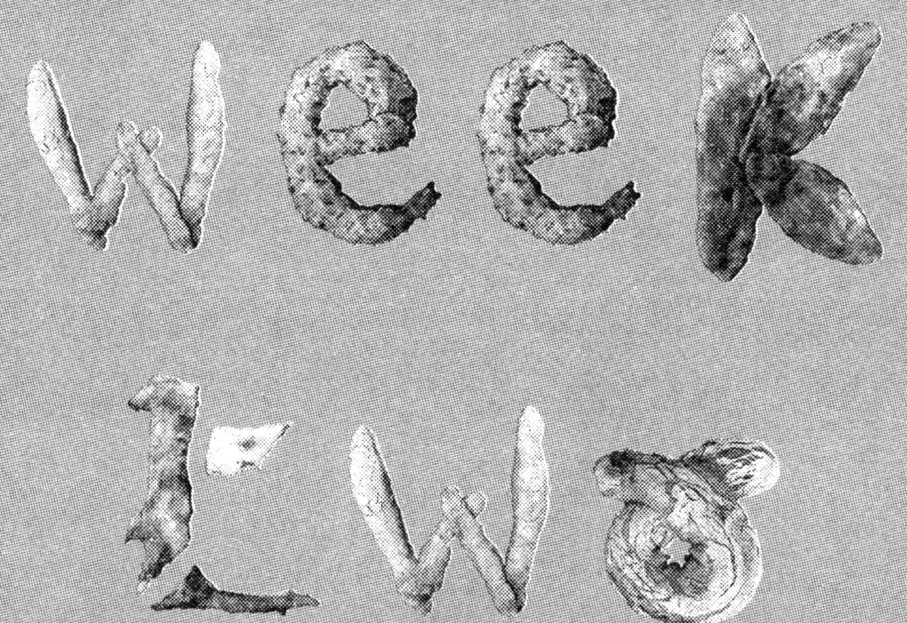
WEEK
TWO

For the second week of the workshop, students were invited to present their ideas and work in progress to the rest of the group.

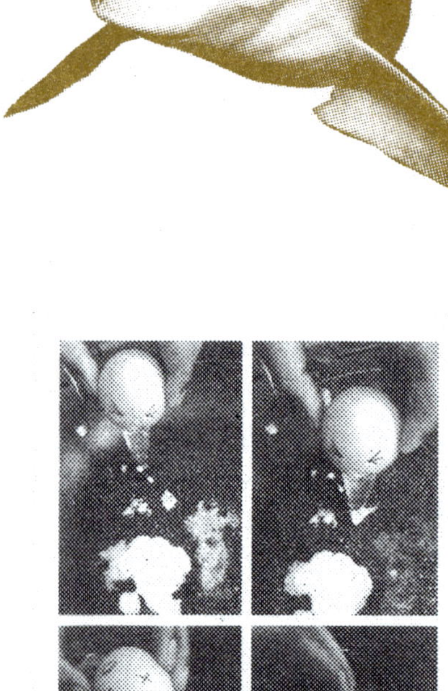

First the group went around looking at each other's sketchbooks, using post-it notes to give constructive specific comments

Preparatory work by, from top to bottom:
(this page) Finley, Habibat Alabi, Kennedy, Charlie
(right hand page)
Sammi, James, and Finley

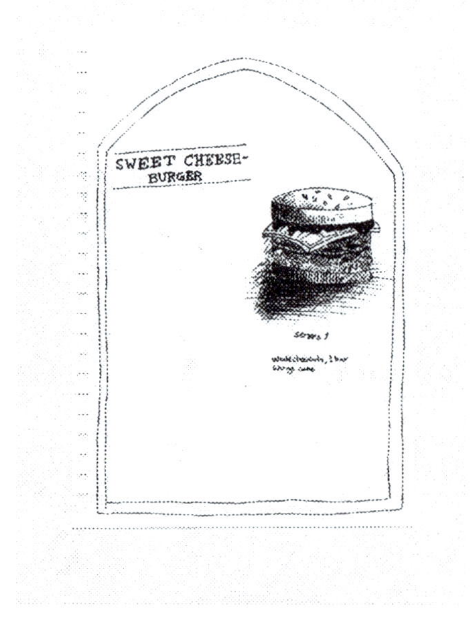

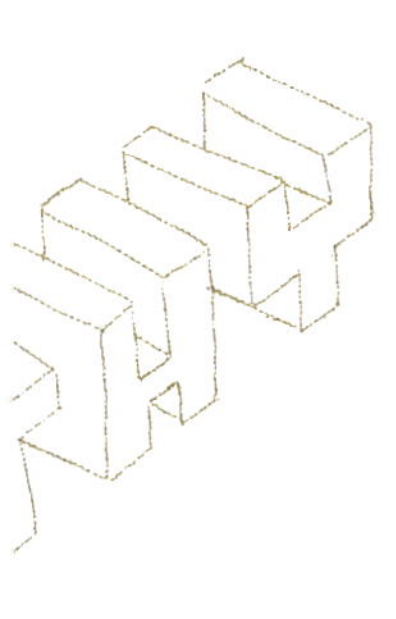

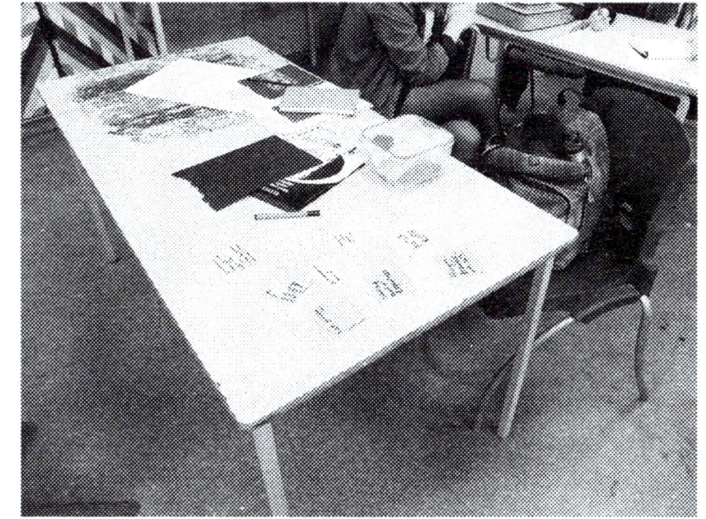

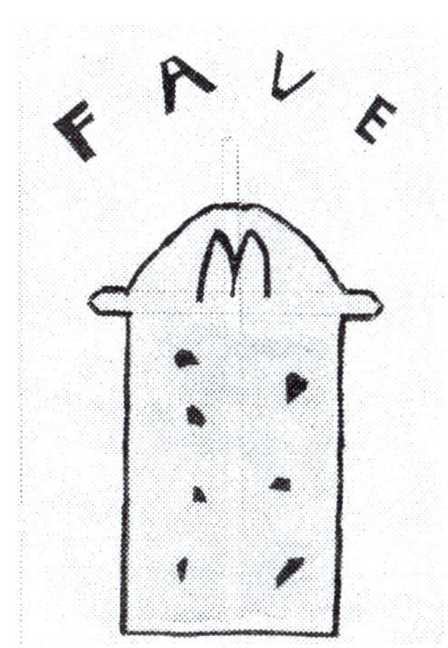
FAVE

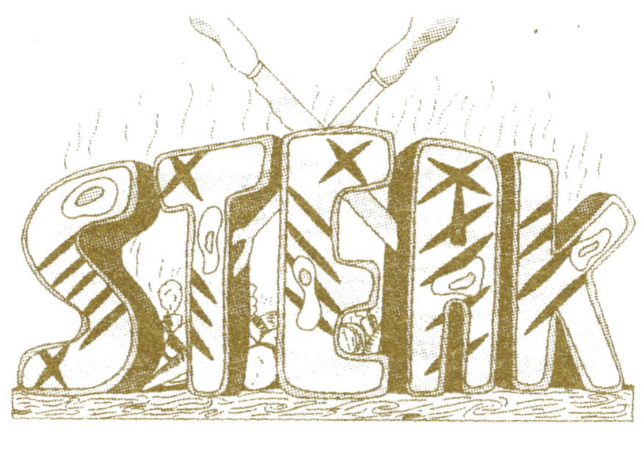
STEAK

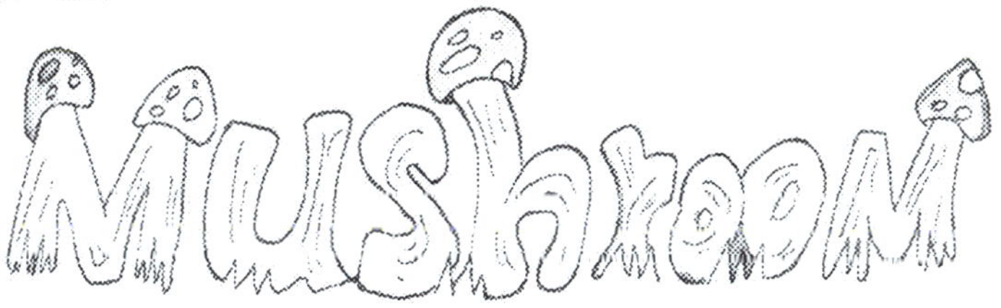
Mushroom

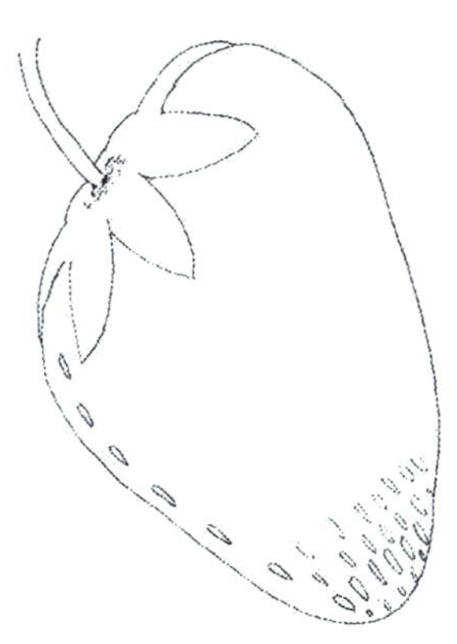

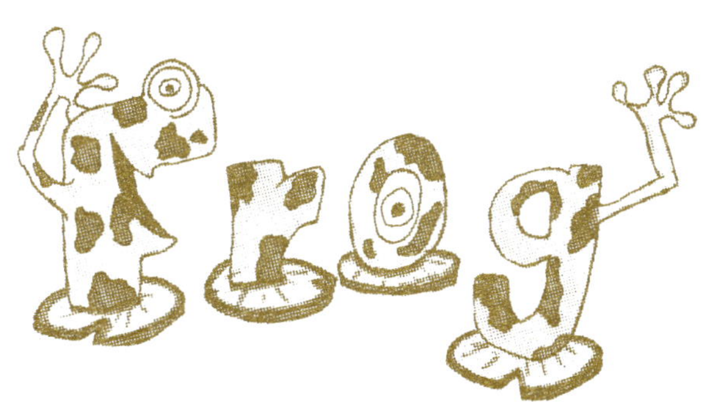
frog

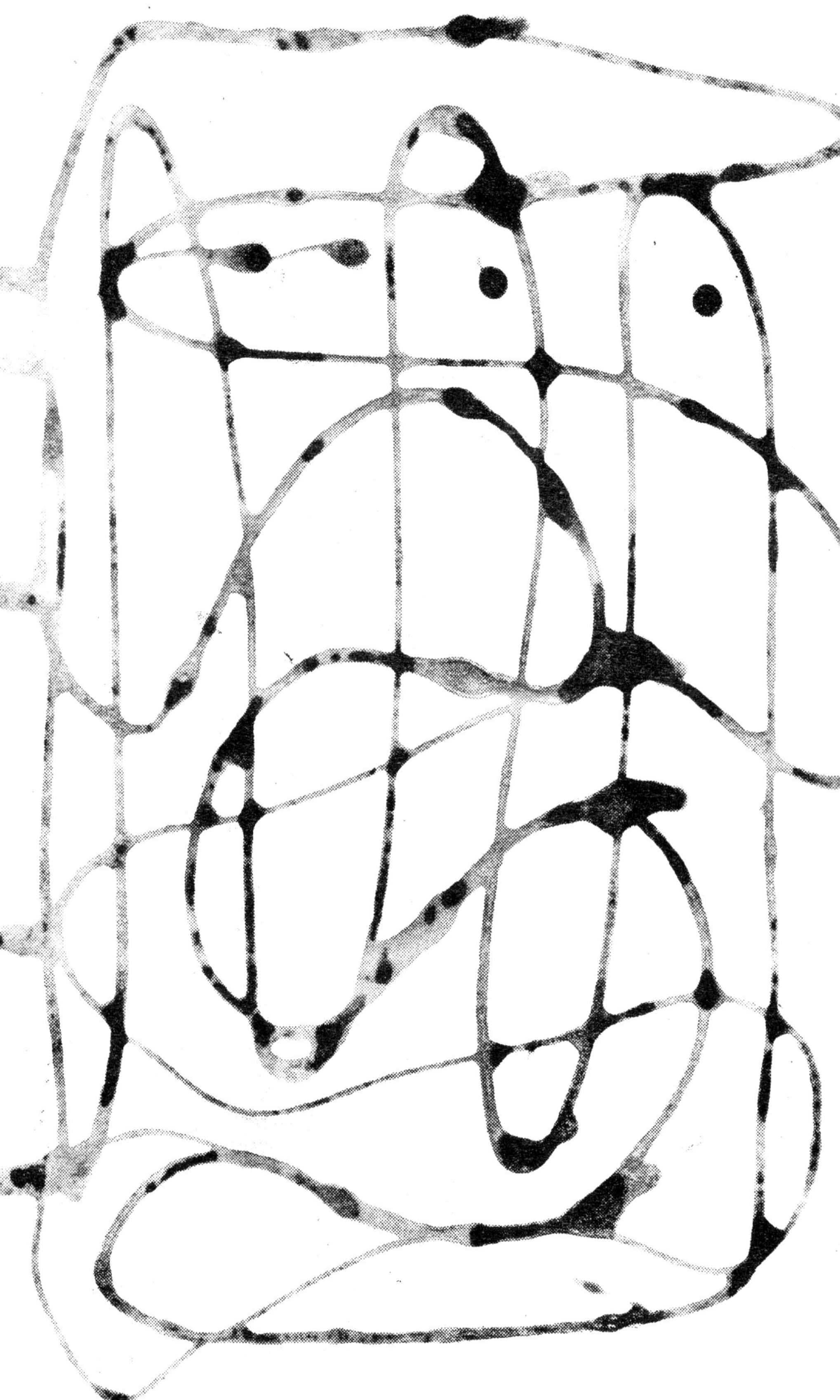

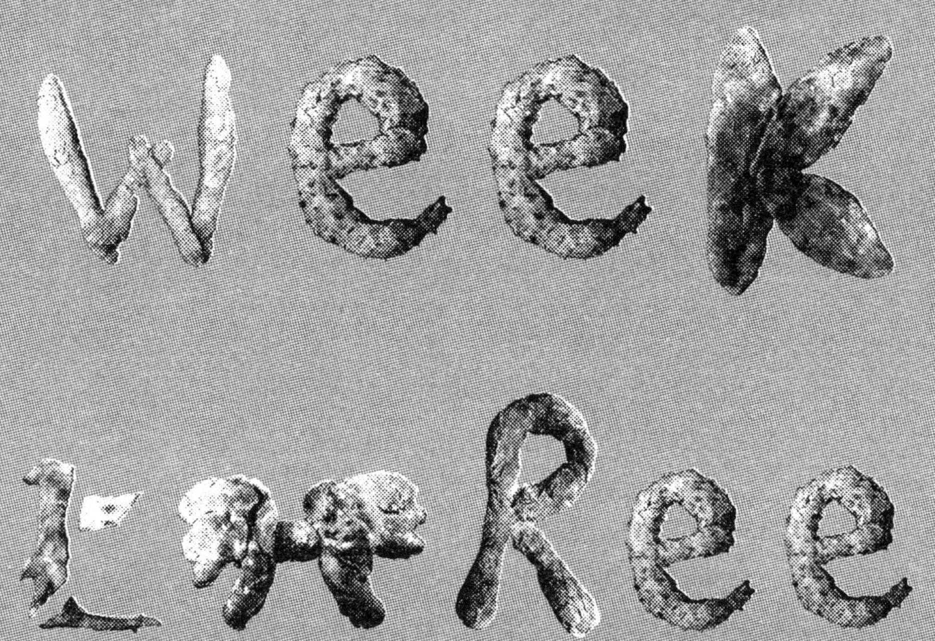

WEEK
THREE

about Riso

Risograph printing – whose output sits between photocopy and screenprinting – has a history of being used by political parties, schools, clubs and organisations since its 1986 release in

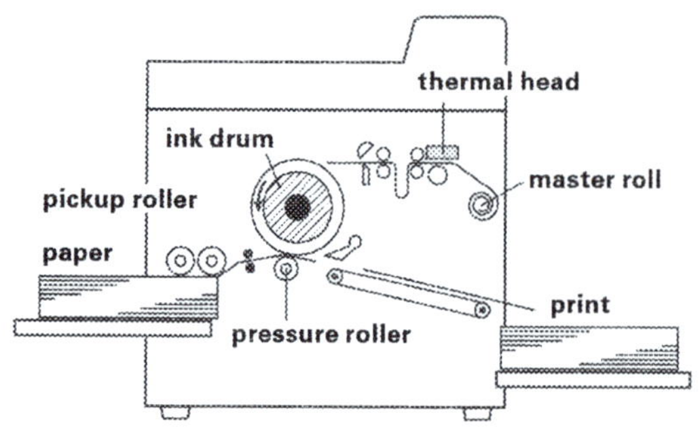

Japan, since it is an ideal process for producing multiple copies quickly and cheaply, at a minimal cost to the environment. Riso is a stencil duplication process, where a master is made from an original image within the machine

and is wrapped around a colour ink drum. Layers of colour can be built up and overlaid in a range of spot colours.

We brought our RP 3700 to Welling, showing the students how to make prints of their work. Firstly they tried a one-colour print, but as the day went on the students gained an understanding of what was possible and began making increasingly complicated prints, a small queue of them forming in front of it with large piles of things to try. During lunch, the teachers were asking to use it to print out things too.

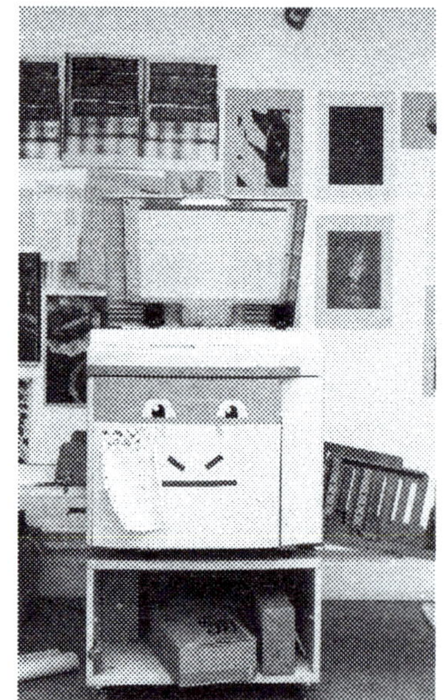

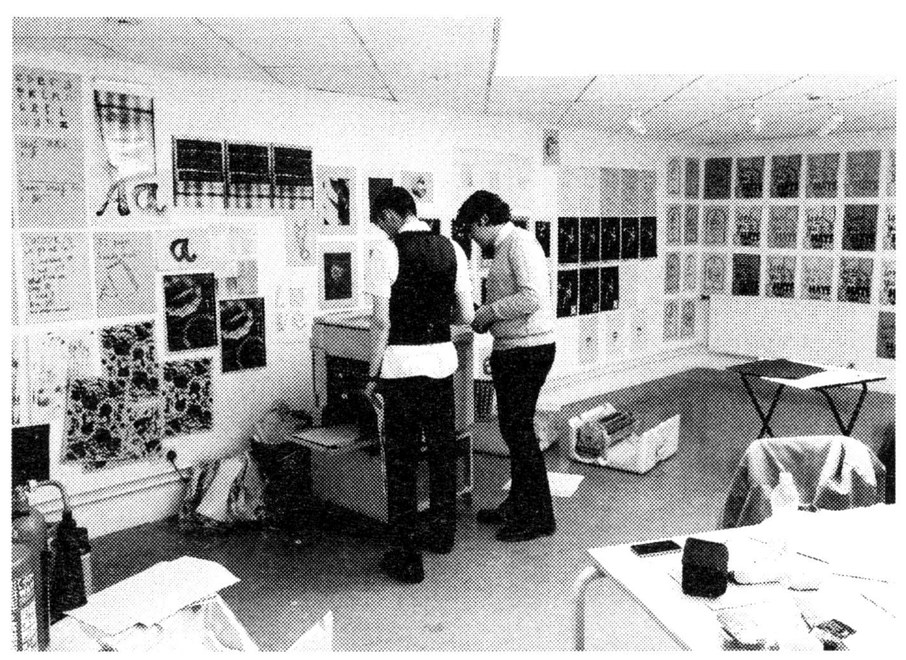

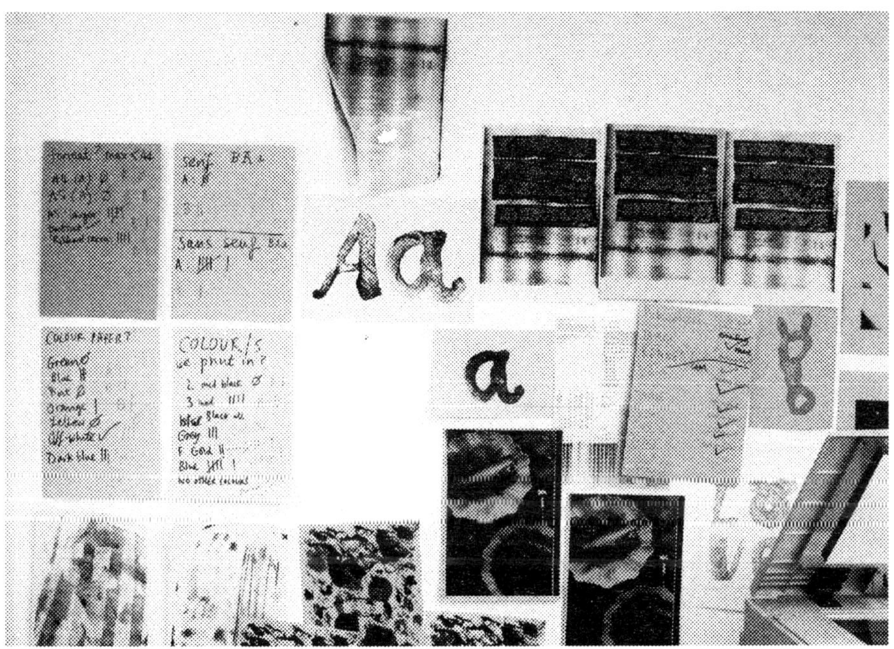

As well as the riso tutorial, in the final week of the workshop there was a group vote to decide on the editorial decisions for this publication, including: what two colours we should use (flat gold and black), what format the book should be (150 x 250mm, slightly taller than A5), what colour paper we should use and whether a serif or sans serif typeface should be used.

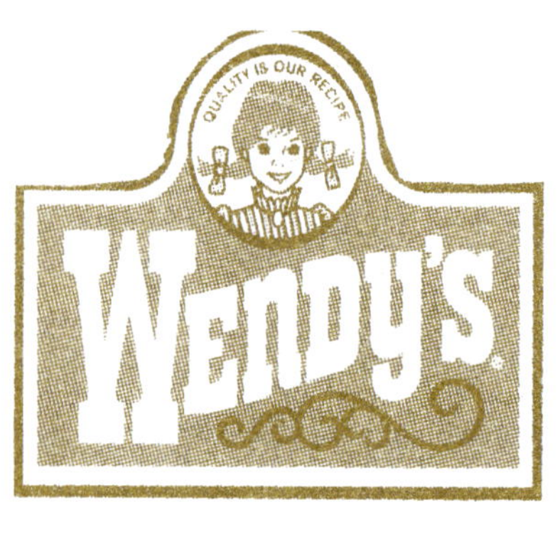
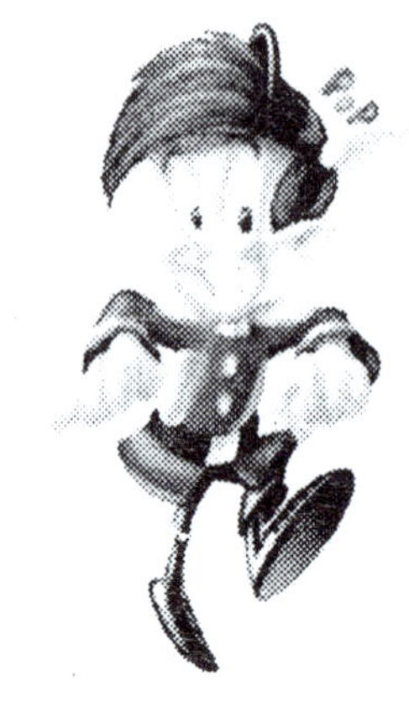
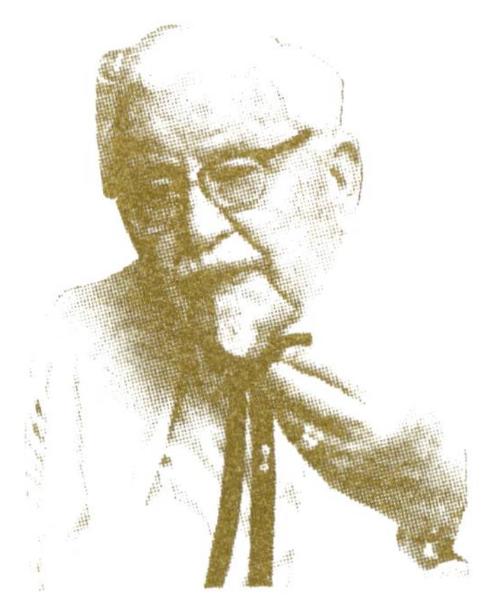
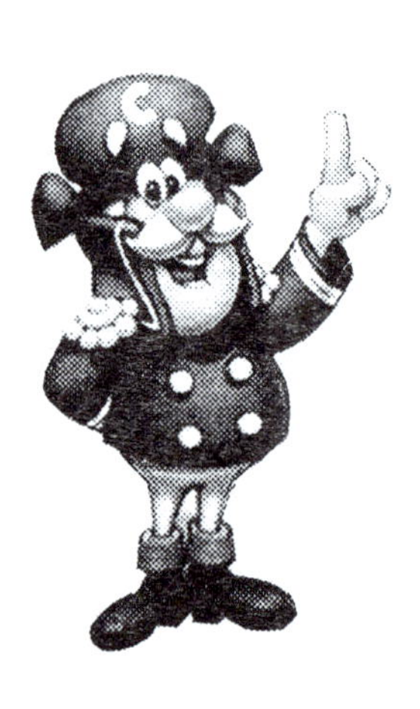
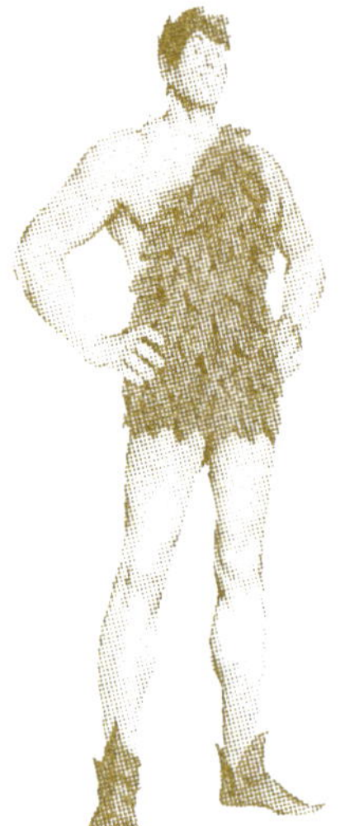
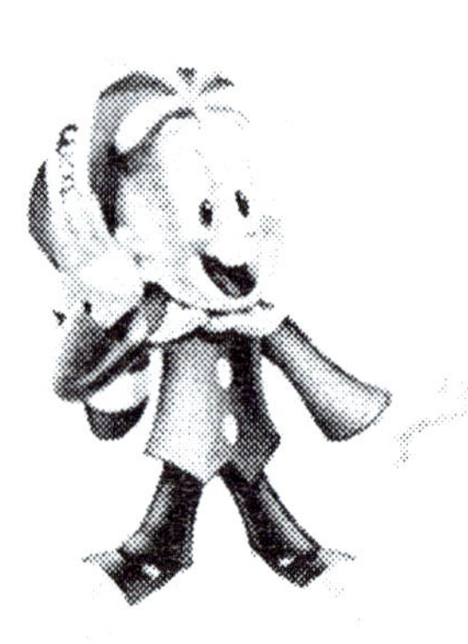
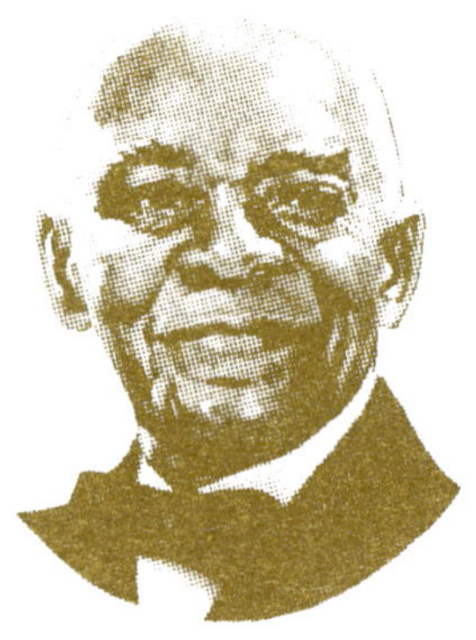
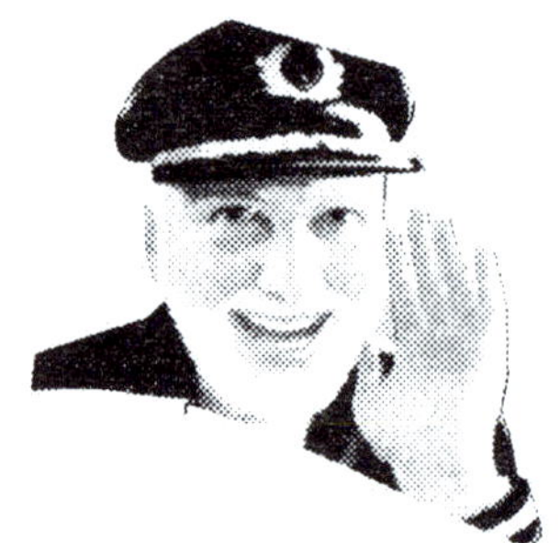

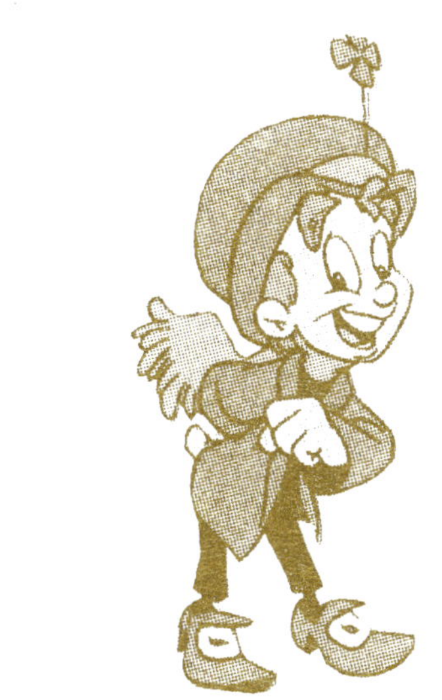

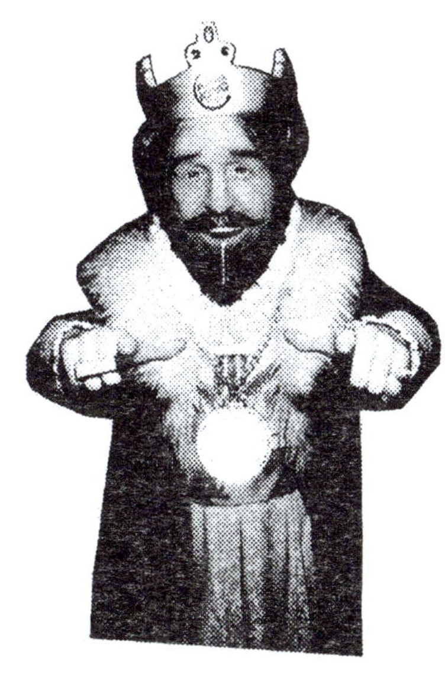

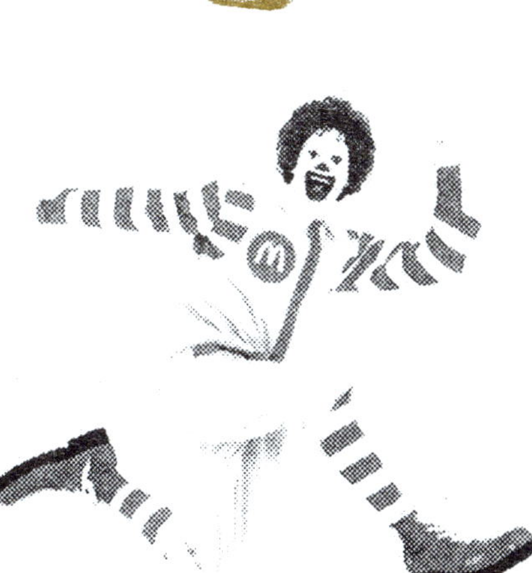

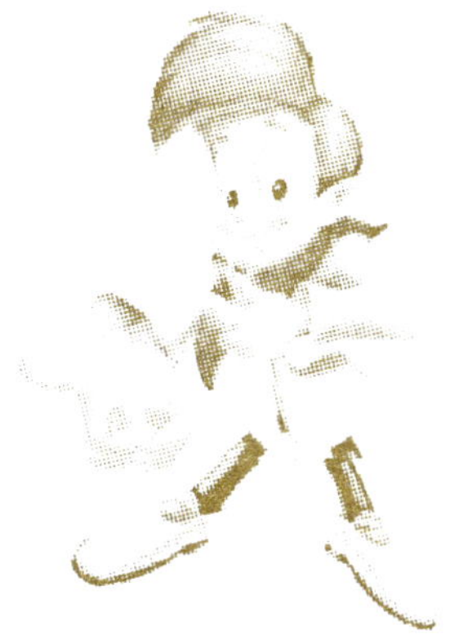

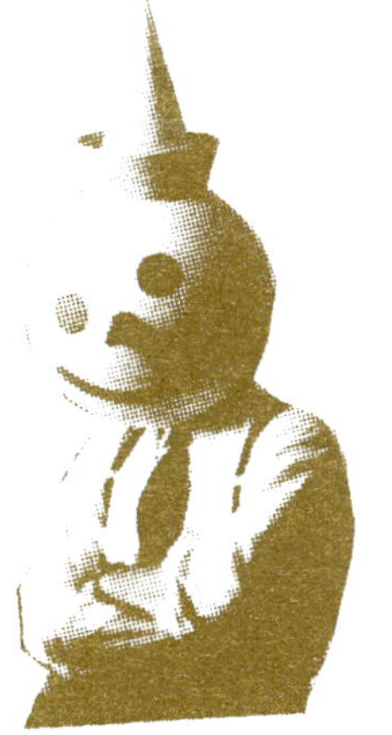

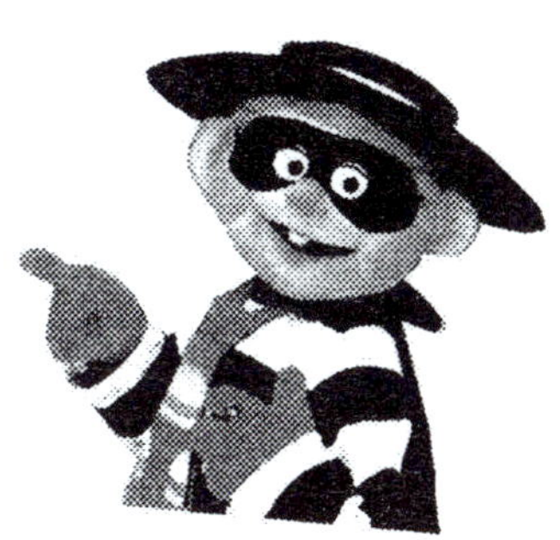

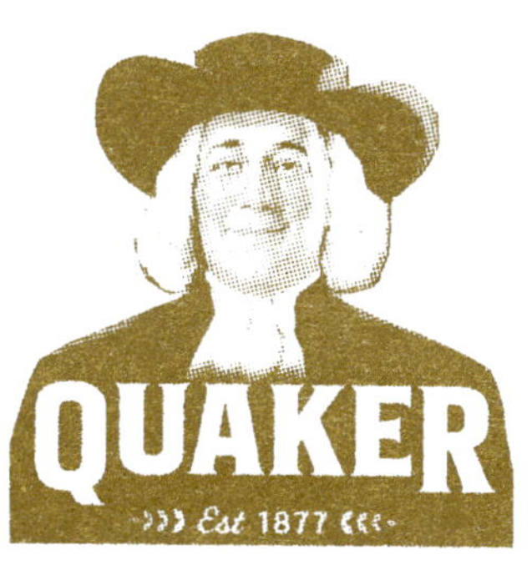
QUAKER
>>> Est 1877 <<<

taste
you
HATE

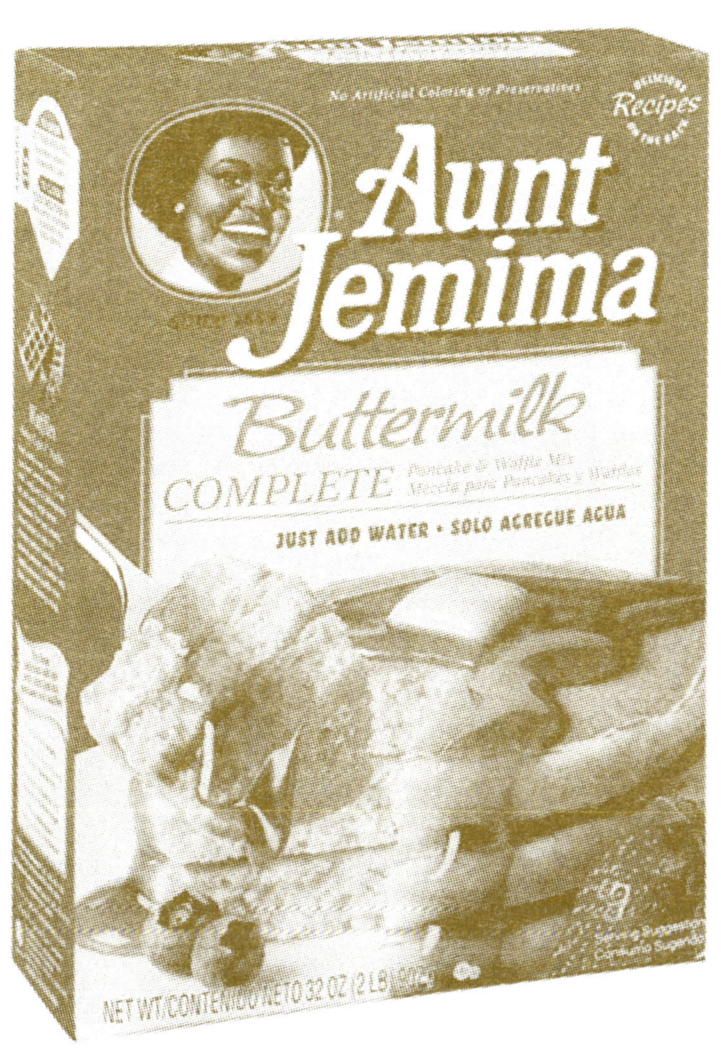
No Artificial Coloring or Preservatives
Recipes
Aunt
Jemima
Buttermilk
COMPLETE
JUST ADD WATER · SOLO AGREGUE AGUA
NET WT/CONTENIDO NETO 32 OZ (2 LB)

OF FOOD WASTE FOOD WASTE OF FOOD WASTE FOOD WASTE OF FOOD

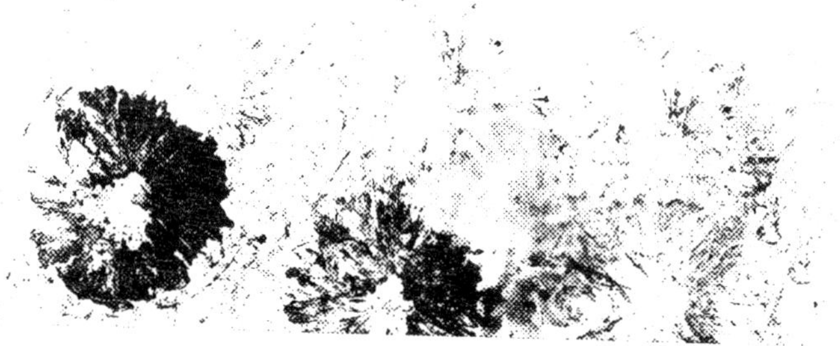

OF FOOD WASTE FOOD WASTE OF FOOD WASTE FOOD WASTE OF FOOD O

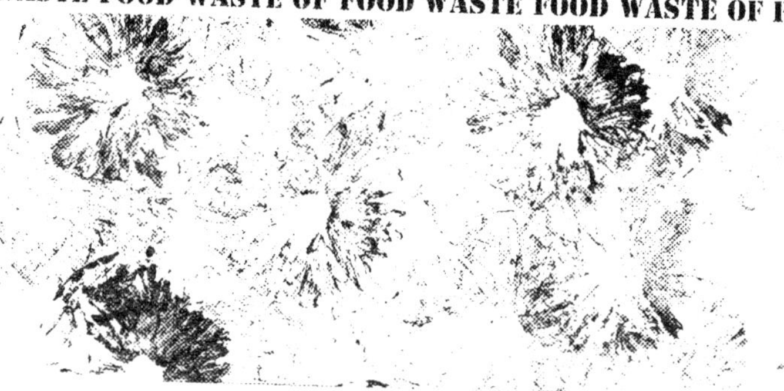

'OOD WASTE FOOD WASTE OF FOOD WASTE FOOD WASTE OF FOOD WASTE

WASTE FOOD WASTE OF FOOD WASTE FOOD WASTE OF FOOD WASTE

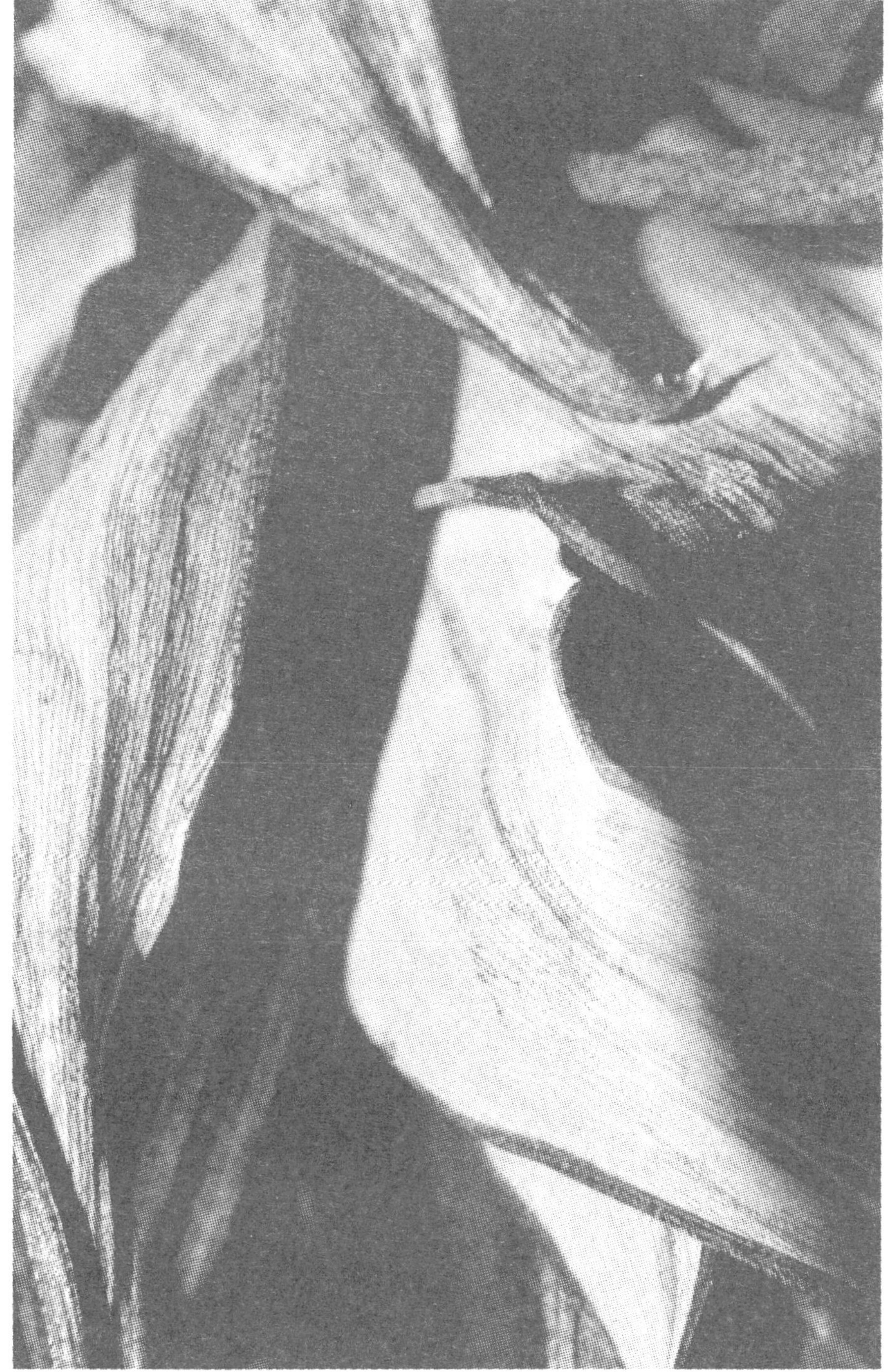

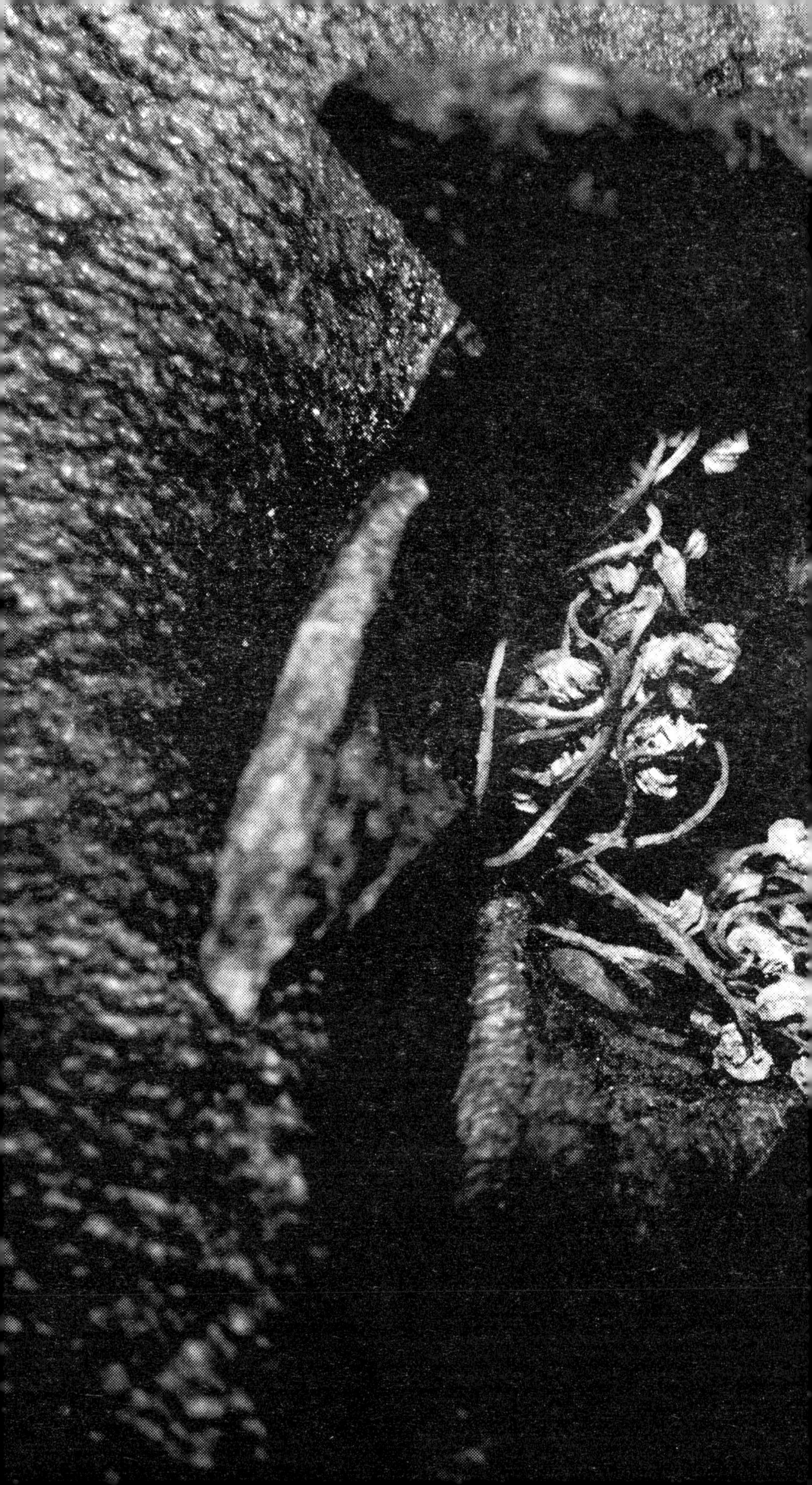

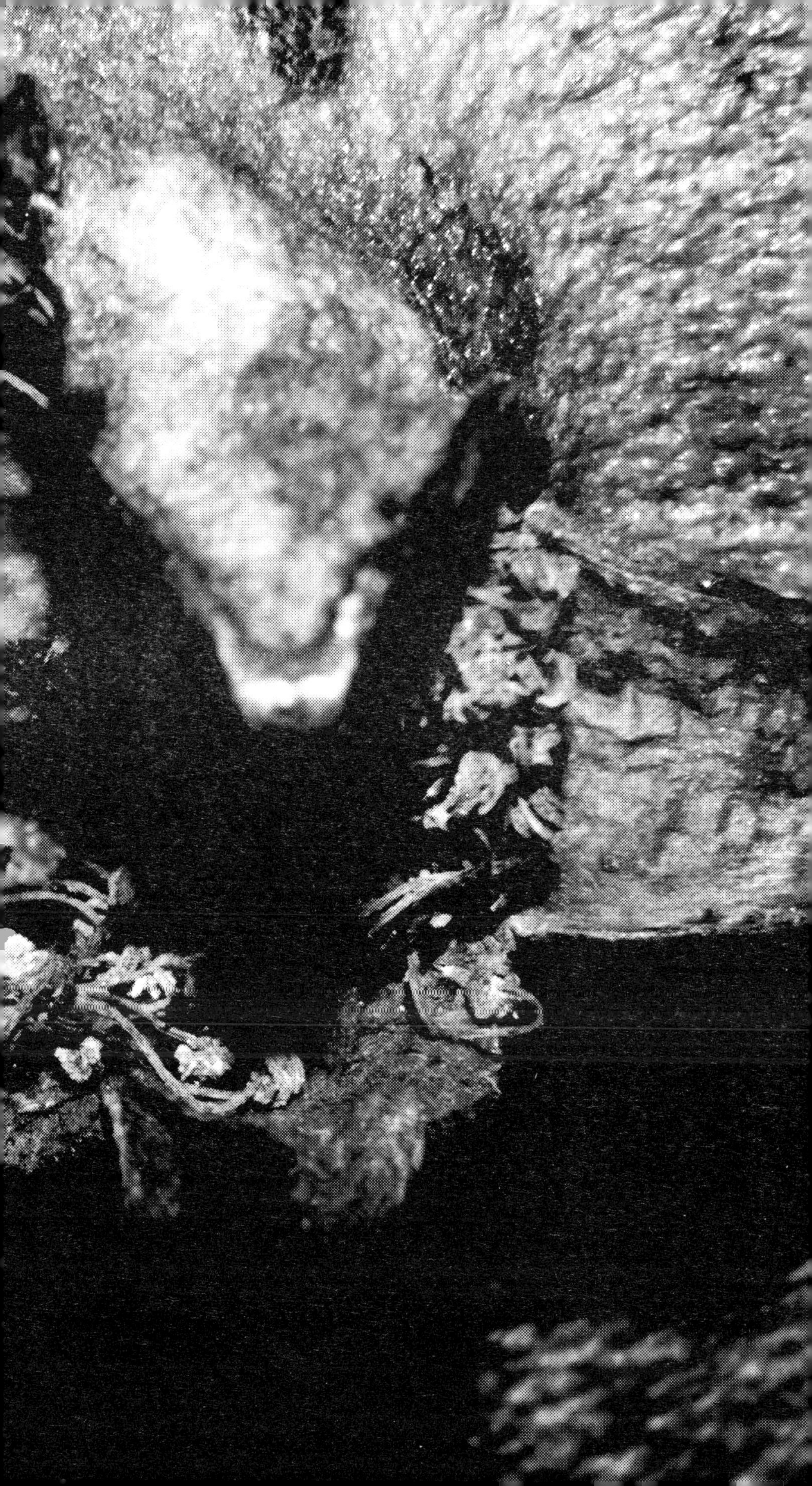

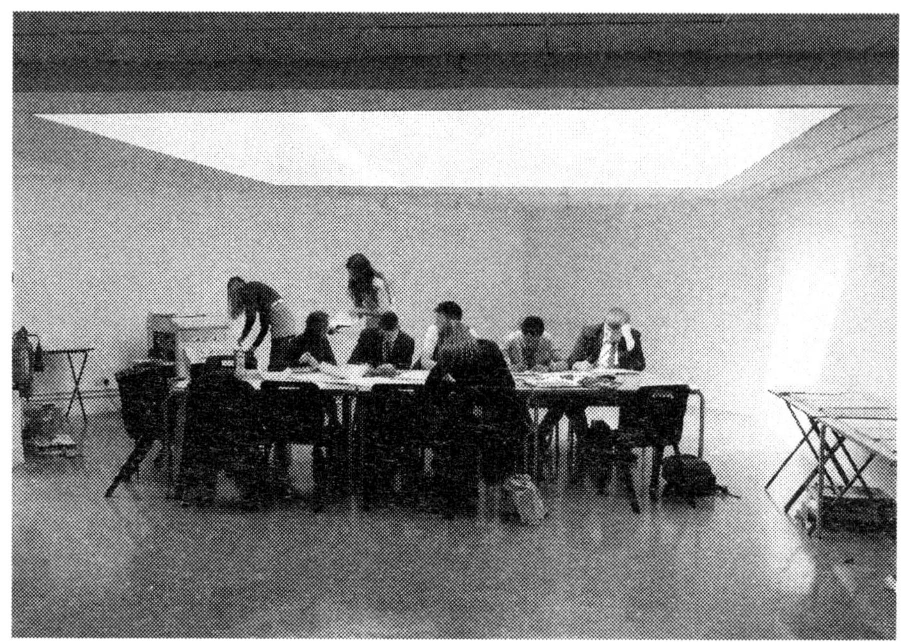

To coincide with the opening of the exhibition *Love Letter to Typography* in the school gallery the students displayed their riso prints, putting them up on the wall as they made them. Some colonised certain parts of the space, others spread theirs out; the collective aim being to cover the walls and take over the gallery as a working print shop and space for experimentation.

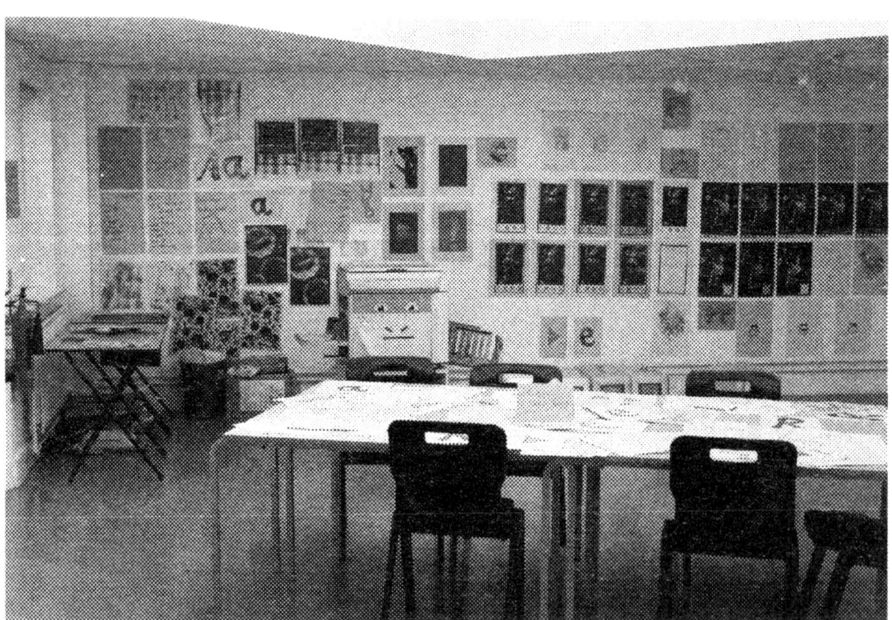

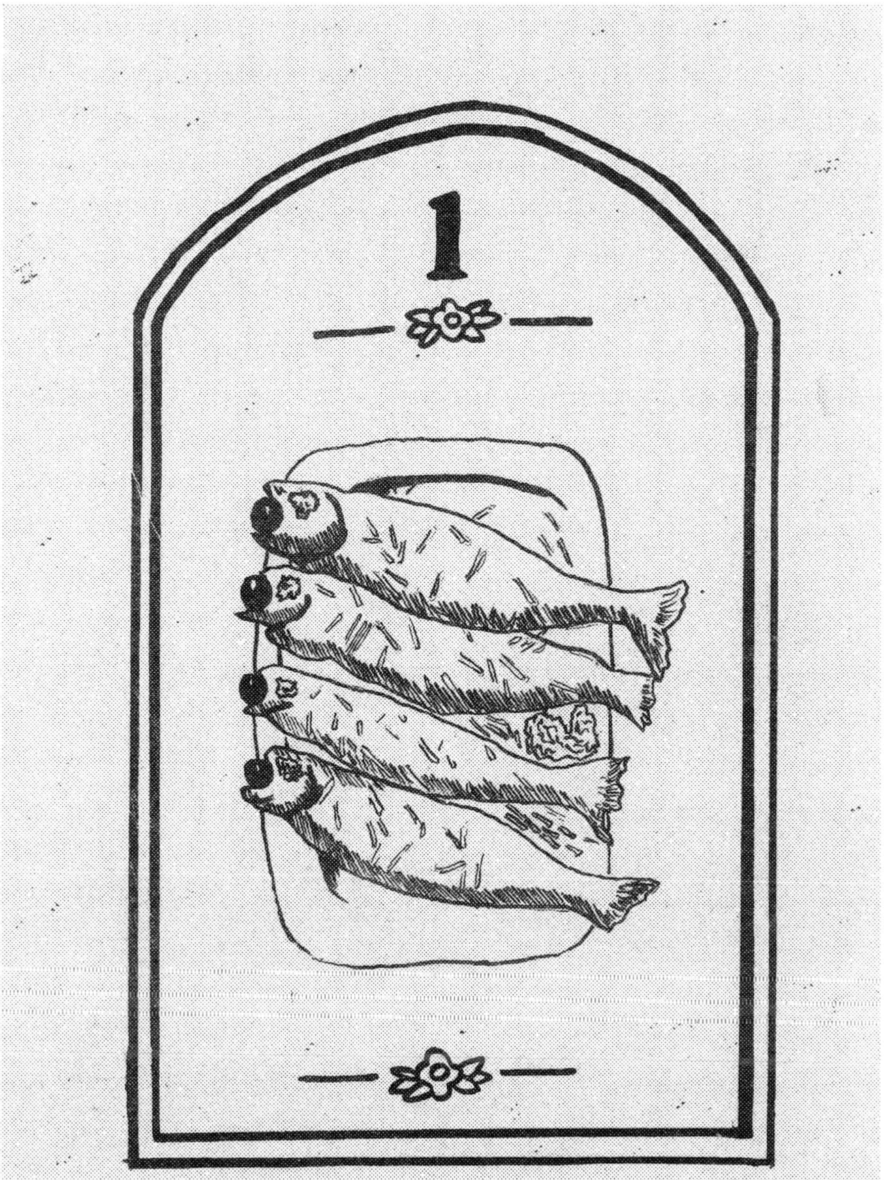

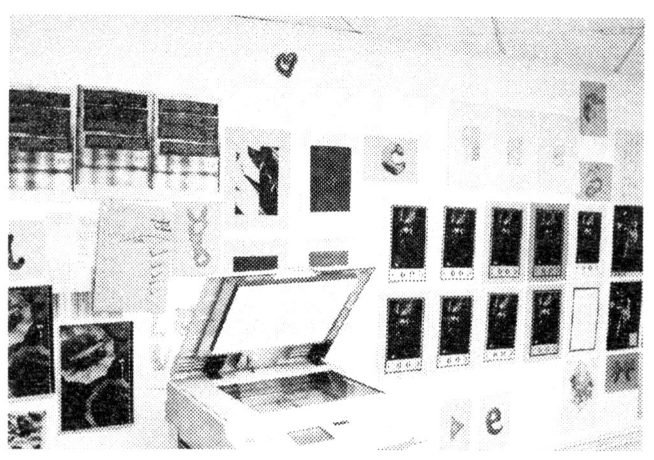

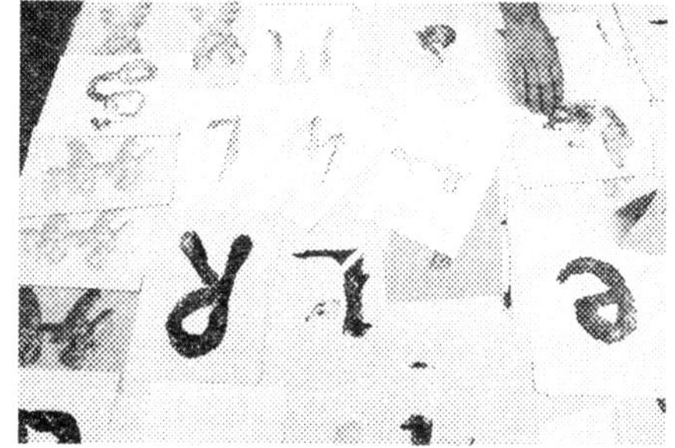

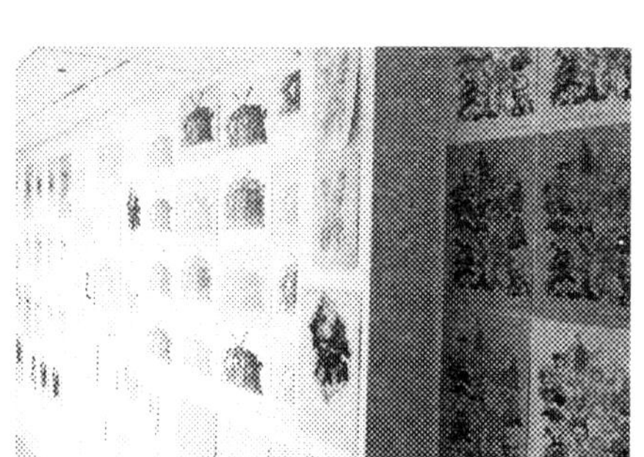

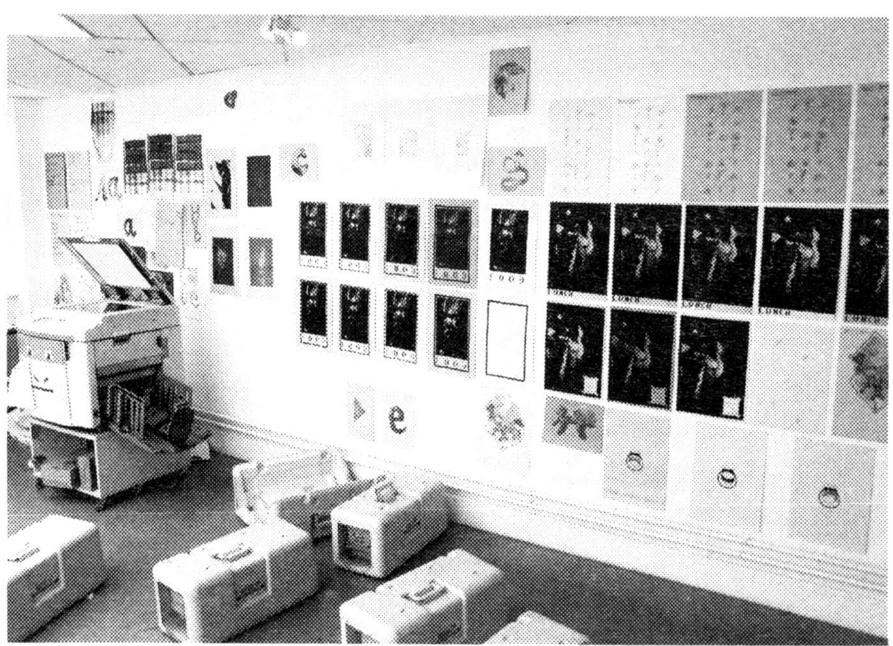

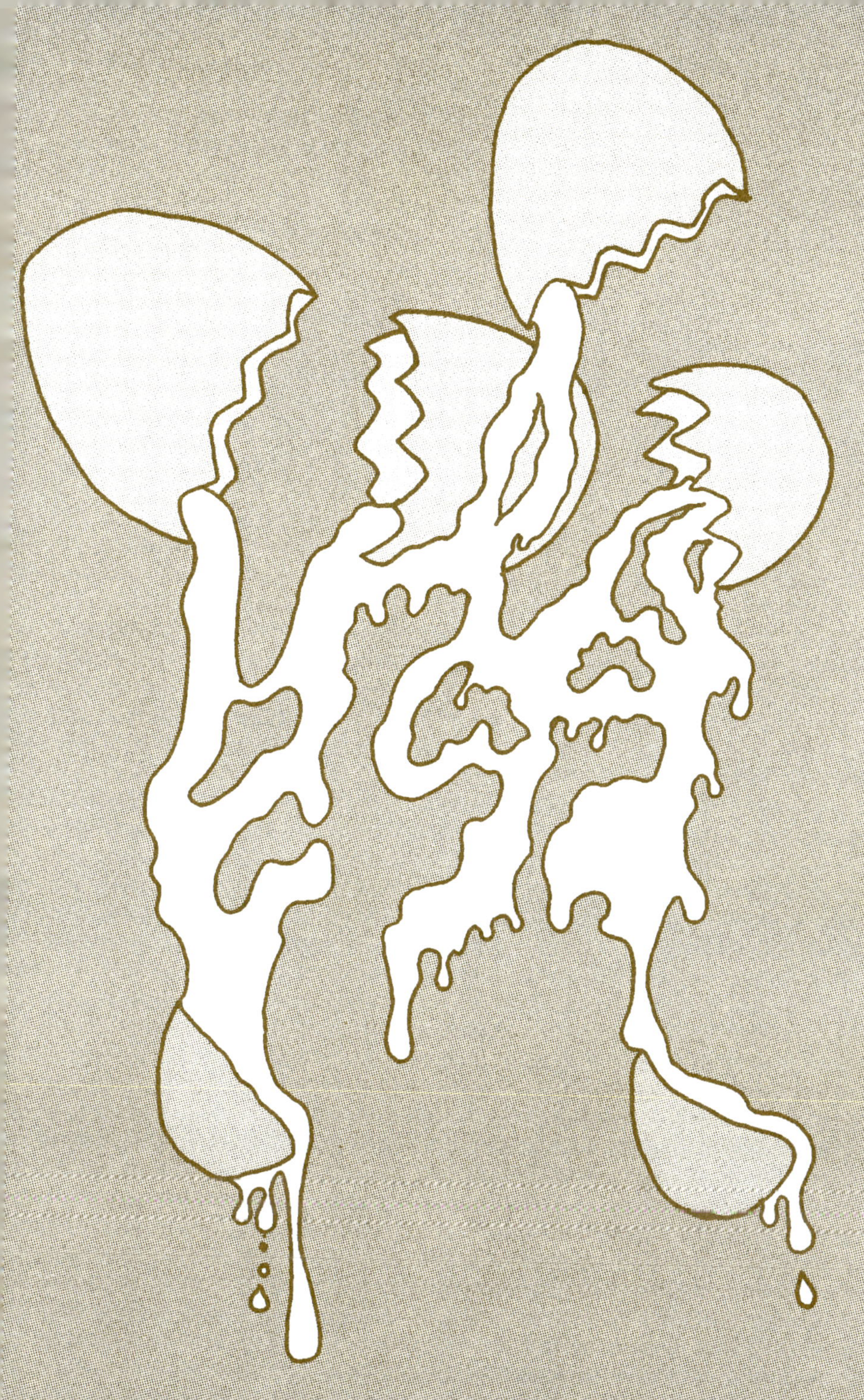

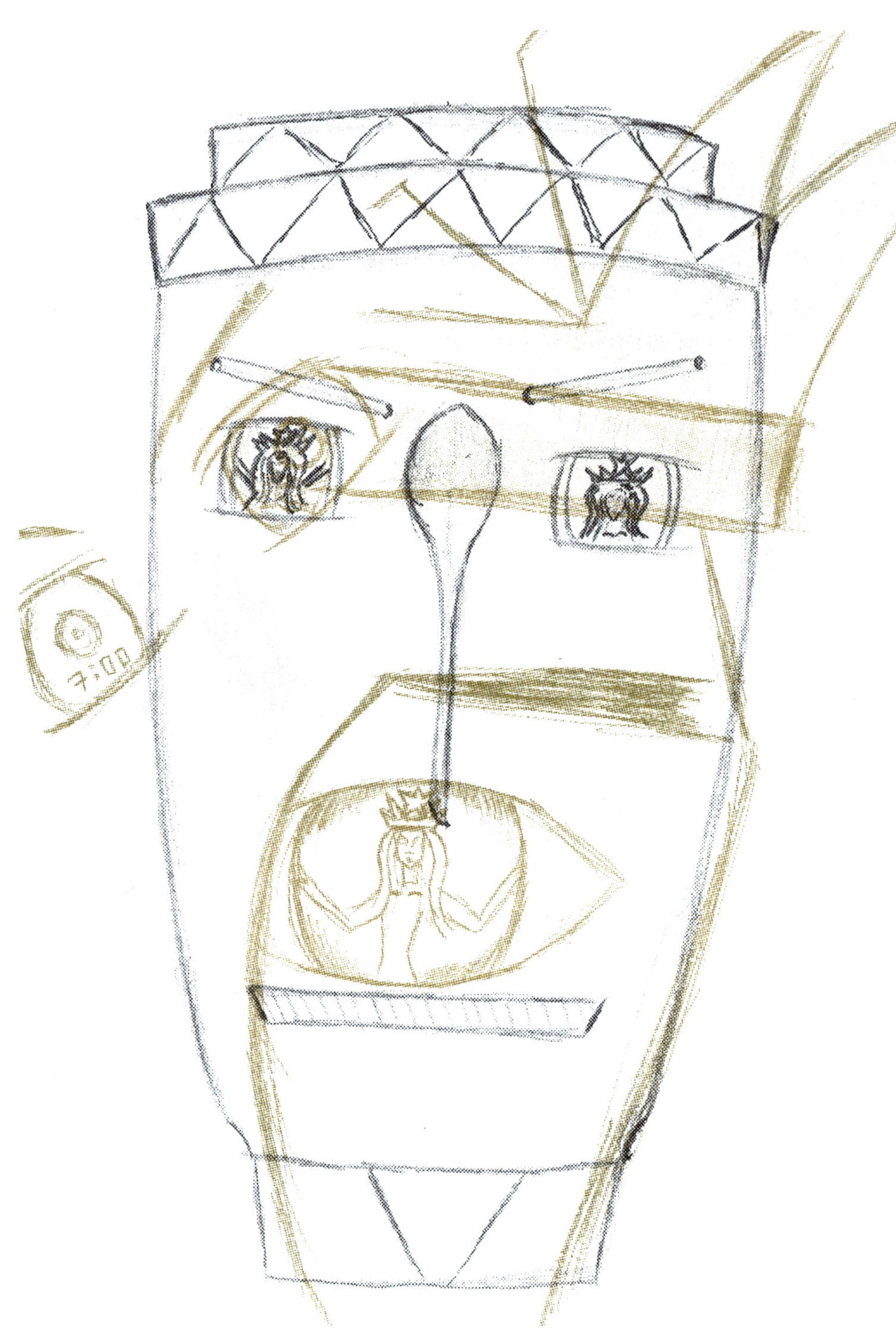
7:00